The Care Manifesto

The Politics of Interdependence

The Care Collective

Andreas Chatzidakis, Jamie Hakim, Jo Littler,
Catherine Rottenberg, and Lynne Segal

VERSO
London • New York

This edition published by Verso 2026
First published by Verso 2020

The manufacturer's authorized representative in the EU for product safety (GPSR) is LOGOS EUROPE, 9 rue Nicolas Poussin, 17000, La Rochelle, France Contact@logoseurope.eu

1 3 5 7 9 10 8 6 4 2

Verso
UK: 6 Meard Street, London W1F 0EG
US: 207 East 32nd Street, New York, NY 10016
versobooks.com

Verso is the imprint of New Left Books

ISBN-13: 978-1-83674-356-9
ISBN-13: 978-1-83976-097-6 (UK EBK)
ISBN-13: 978-1-83976-098-3 (US EBK)

British Library Cataloguing in Publication Data
A catalogue record for this book is available from the British Library

Library of Congress Cataloging-in-Publication Data
A catalog record for the previous edition of this book is available from the Library of Congress

Typeset in Sabon by Biblichor Ltd, Edinburgh
Printed and bound by CPI Group (UK) Ltd, Croydon CR0 4YY

Contents

Preface

Six years ago, Verso published the first edition of *The Care Manifesto*. It was a small volume that provided a large overview of what we described as the reigning neoliberal politics of 'structural carelessness'. We suggested that care should not be understood as a moral virtue in and of itself, but rather as the necessary condition for life; and, as our subtitle put it, as based around a 'politics of interdependence'. The manifesto unpacked the different meanings of care, highlighting past and present examples of progressive practice, and offered a vision of an alternative future organised around the politics of care on multiple scales, from the intimate to the planetary.

When the manifesto appeared, it hit a nerve. We had finished writing it just as the Covid-19 pandemic erupted. By the time the book was published, we were in the midst of a lockdown in the UK, where we are all currently based, despite hailing from different parts of the world. During these early months, 'care talk' was appearing everywhere – from directives to 'take care' to the weekly 'clap for carers'. For so many, there was a shared sense that the world was in profound crisis and that, collectively, we urgently needed to flip the dominant cultural, political and economic scripts on their heads.

It became evident very quickly just how unprepared the world had been for a pandemic, despite years of warnings that precisely such a scenario was possible. Even in richer countries like the UK and the US, many hospitals were already under-resourced and under-staffed; thus, when the pandemic hit, they had to operate with extreme shortages of personal protective equipment (PPE). This was soon compounded by hasty commissions from wholly unvetted and inadequate suppliers, many of whom we soon discovered had personal connections to individuals in government and profited massively from these contracts.

At the time, all of this meant that there was a distinct feeling that the world had entered a transitional moment in which there was a window of opportunity to begin 'building back better' and when real change seemed possible. We had also just witnessed the speed at which governments could, if they so wished, transform national priorities while imposing unprecedented lock-downs to prevent the spread of Covid-19. And while some of the care talk during the first years of the pandemic – such as the UK government applauding care workers – was primarily performative, demonstrating 'care gratitude' rather than 'care justice', a great deal of it – especially that coming from the grassroots – was genuine, and provided hope that another, more egalitarian future was indeed possible.[1]

To our surprise, the book quickly sold tens of thousands of copies, reaching a global audience. With the pandemic shifting many conversations online, we found ourselves talking about *The Care Manifesto* and about the practices and meanings of care with many different people around the world. There was and continues to be a flourishing diversity of groups and networks involved with practicing, theorising, and reimagining care in creative ways, as the book highlights.

It has has been energising and inspiring to connect with so many of them: from local political meetings and international union solidarity conferences, through academic care theory networks and mutual aid workers, to individual podcasters and national media outlets. Our manifesto has now been translated into over a dozen languages, and the vision of a world organised around care that it lays out has connected with and been adopted in a multitude of forms, venues, and locations.

The notion of 'universal care' we popularised has inspired museum and gaming exhibitions as well as theatre productions across the UK, Europe, and beyond. Youth groups, community organisations, grassroots collectives, and NGOs have contacted us and incorporated our approach to care as part of their curricula and political platforms. There has also been significant scholarly engagement with the manifesto's key ideas and claims, with articles and journal issues dedicated to discussing how we define care and our feminist, queer, anti-racist, and eco-socialist utopian vision.[2]

Of course, there has also been some important criticism. There were inevitably other examples we could have used or areas we could have focused on. Some scholars and activists have raised concerns that our understanding of care may be too expansive, suggesting that such a capacious conception and practice of care might weaken its existing explanatory and descriptive precision.

Pointing to the universal nature of our care needs, these critics worry, might undermine struggles or campaigns in support of more specific care needs for highly vulnerable groups. However, in response to this critique, we still argue that good care at any one scale or level is inextricably dependent upon broader issues relating to care at all of the other levels. For instance, providing adequate care for children, especially in poorer households, requires caring communities with easy access to parks, playgrounds, and free nurseries. But for local communities to maintain such resources, there needs to be a caring state rather than a state squeezing local government in order to save money.

Meanwhile, caring states can only exist when not impoverished by debt, which takes us to global issues such as transnational wealth redistribution and debt relief for poorer countries. The ability to care at one scale really is dependent upon possibilities for provision at another, as well as on the need to recognise our global interdependencies. The realities of climate crises along with the threat of future pandemics and the increased displacement of populations produced by expanding zones of conflict should all remind us of our complex interconnections which need to be acknowledged and addressed if we are to prioritise the creation of a caring and sustainable world.

~

Five years on from the publication of our manifesto, we find ourselves in a very different political reality. Indeed, we are in the middle of what we would describe as a radical and accelerated process of 'care-stripping'.[3] This involves the systematic dismantling of almost all of our remaining public care resources and provisions in order to turbocharge profit for a handful of billionaires and financialised corporations. It involves dumping models of progressive care by governments which are, today, either run by these billionaires or who fear and pander to them. Adequate care is increasingly restricted to those with the financial resources to pay for it (already a diminishing group), evident in the exponential increase of the marketised care economy promising large 'returns of investment'.[4]

In the UK, for instance, rights and resources for disabled people are under attack. We are also seeing the growing use of AI and robotics technology which, when used in a corporate care context, often leads to less interpersonal contact and more alienation and loneliness. Meanwhile, many corporations are rushing to eliminate any programmes that could be even remotely associated with the idea that they care for anything other than profits. Soon after Trump's second inauguration, there was a full-frontal assault on healthcare, environmental protections, and education, and household brands such as Target, Walmart, Amazon, and Google swiftly scrapped their diversity, equity, and inclusion (DEI) initiatives.

A similar fate awaited environmental and social governance programmes, once the hallmark of so-called 'conscious capitalism'. This has led to major oil companies such as BP, Shell, and Equinor downsizing or ditching their widely broadcast renewable goals and doubling down on fossil fuel extraction, jumping on the Trumpian mantra 'drill, baby, drill'.[5]

So what happened to care? Five years ago, we witnessed what we described as 'a discursive explosion of care' among a remarkably diverse range of actors – from governments and corporations to NGOs and grassroots movements – even as its invocation served radically different agendas: both the disingenuous anti-care of corporate 'carewashing' and the actual care of solidarity, egalitarianism, and co-operation. Fast forward to today, and care talk is no longer so ubiquitous. Indeed, for those right-wing figures who have ascended to power, the opposite is the case. According to Elon Musk, the world's richest billionaire, empathy and care are now 'the fundamental weaknesses of Western civilization'. What might have felt outrageously out of touch only a few years ago now captures a nihilistic streak of the current zeitgeist. Violence, the nemesis of care, is now experiencing an unbearable explosion, not least in Gaza, where Western governments and corporations are shamelessly benefiting from what the UN's Special Rapporteur Francesca Albanese, in her influential 2025 report, described as 'the economy of genocide'.[6] How can we – why would we – foreground care when hate is being positioned, both by billionaires and right-wing politicians, as the cocaine of the people?

Sometimes those responsible for care-stripping still claim to care, albeit differently. In the case of Donald Trump, care is now restricted to 'people like us', mostly white and traditionalist, 'good' Americans longing for a return to a greatness that never was. Meanwhile, those who cannot ignore the diversity of their constituents, such as powerful corporations, have begun practicing linguistic gymnastics. HSBC's Chief Sustainability Officer Julian Wentzel, for instance, has announced that the bank still cares about the planet and will now take a 'more measured approach' to investing in the fossil fuel industry.[7] Underneath such carewashing, a mere pretence of caring, lies a reality that we should never forget and one that even powerful politicians and corporations still find difficult to completely disavow: that care and its practice are necessary for human and non-human life, and that so many of us still care about care.

In our everyday lives and on the ground, care is what so many of us do and strive to improve on a daily basis. We provide care within our households and in our neighbourhoods, struggling to meet the care needs of others while also trying to maintain, against all odds, a certain level of personal physical and mental well-being. At the grassroots level, the appetite for more care and less violence has far from disappeared, evidenced not only in the curricula and exhibitions mentioned above but also in initiatives such as the 'care teams' now regularly employed at queer community events to ensure attendees feel safe and cared for. At the municipal level, for example, Bogotá's Mayor Claudia López introduced the *Manzanas del Cuidado*, or 'care blocks', through which the city temporarily assumes the care duties of unpaid carers, allowing them time to study, play sports, or train for jobs. On a global scale, the extremely popular pro-Palestine demonstrations – where hundreds of thousands have protested weekly since 2023 against the Israeli genocide in Gaza – and the related resurgence of the BDS movement further reflect the desire for a world rooted in care as opposed to one marked by growing cruelty and violence.

If anything, then, the current landscape often seems to mark an unprecedented disconnect between the many care projects on the ground and care's disavowal by so many of those in positions of financial and institutional power. Those centrist and right-wing actors with the most political power who could ensure access to care at all levels and help put a decisive end to all forms of collective violence are failing to accept any such obligation. Instead, they favour promoting predatory extractive capitalism, environmental destruction, and personal greed. These actions are even more stark and outrageous today than before Covid-19, when we began writing this manifesto. While we saw the urgency surrounding every aspect of care five years ago, today more and more social care sectors are teetering on the brink of collapse, and whole populations are being subjected to genocidal violence. Our collective failure to care at the most basic level – namely, hands-on care for the most vulnerable – tells us that the reign of carelessness and the politics of violence and cruelty have intensified.

Yet, even as it does seem that we are further away from realizing the goal of placing care at the centre of our politics, care remains as powerful, as necessary, and as fundamental as ever. Moreover, as we state in this manifesto, it is crucial to recognise that creating socialised forms of care is always a struggle, one that has to involve democratic movements and actors working on multiple levels and scales, including, of course, gaining political power. These seeds of hope are not absent: there are inspiring examples – from redistribution in Mexico to the election of Mamdani in New York – of some blooming. As this manifesto outlines, we constantly need to reinvigorate and reinvent the goal of placing care at the centre of all our kinship networks, communities, economies, states, and politics. We urgently need to exceed the energies of the care-stripping classes by building our collective, interdependent solidarity and political power. We need to replace 'fascist passions' with caring passions.[8] We can do this by borrowing from old and new strategies, acting across all scales of life, and by collaborating – in myriad inventive ways – with all those who know, or hope, that another, better world is still possible, and who keep pushing to bring it about.

The Care Collective
January 2026

Introduction: Carelessness Reigns

Our world is one in which carelessness reigns. The coronavirus pandemic merely highlights this ongoing carelessness in many countries, including the USA, the UK and Brazil. These countries dismissed early warnings about the very real and imminent threat of pandemics to come, choosing instead to waste billions on military hardware against distant or non-existent threats and to funnel money to the already rich. This has meant those most at risk from Covid-19 – health workers, social carers, the elderly, those with underlying health conditions, the poor, the incarcerated, and the precariously employed – have received negligible help or support, while lessons that could have been shared on the best ways for protecting them have been largely ignored.

Yet long before the pandemic, care services had already been slashed and priced out of reach for many of the elderly and disabled, hospitals were routinely overwhelmed and in crisis, homelessness had been on the rise for years, and increasing numbers of schools had begun dealing with pupil hunger. Meanwhile, multinational corporations had been making huge profits out of financialising and overleveraging care homes while work in the care sector was subsumed into the corporate gig economy, making precarious workers not only more numerous but also hugely overstretched, vulnerable and thus less able to care.

At the same time, over the past few decades, ideas of social welfare and community had been pushed aside for individualised notions of resilience, wellness and self-improvement, promoted through a ballooning 'self-care' industry which relegates care to something we are supposed to buy for ourselves on a personal basis. This offers a wholly insufficient sticking plaster for these problems. In short, for a long time we had simply been failing to care for each other, especially the vulnerable, the poor and the weak.

It has tragically taken a worldwide pandemic to remind us of just how vital robust care services are. Moreover, Covid-19 has compelled many of us to adopt new forms of taking care – from mutual aid to social distancing and self-isolation. All around the globe, from New York to London, Athens, and Delhi, people clap every week to demonstrate support for essential care workers. Rhetorically at least, governments worldwide have responded, and in sharp contrast to 2019, *talk* of care is currently everywhere. Even the least likely have rolled out major economic aid packages in the name of care for the nation. Surprising though these actions may have been, the aid packages have not been enough to counteract the decades of organised neglect suffered by our caring infrastructures and economies more generally. Moreover, recent analysis has shown that in too many countries these packages are tailored mostly to the benefit of the wealthy; in some cases, these seemingly progressive efforts actively work to disguise the fascist policies of those administering them. India's Hindu-nationalist prime minister Narendra Modi outdid even his peers, introducing a welfare package called 'PM Cares' as he continued to orchestrate the brutal clampdown on Kashmir and the delegitimisation of Muslim migrant workers.

So, although we are hearing much more about care in these unsettling days, carelessness continues to reign. Our manifesto is written to redress this lack of care.

The crisis of care has become particularly acute over the last forty years, as governments accepted neoliberal capitalism's near-ubiquitous positioning of profit-making as the organising principle of life. It has meant systematically prioritising the interests and flows of financial capital, while ruthlessly dismantling welfare states and democratic processes and institutions. As we have seen, this kind of market logic has led to the austerity policies that have significantly reduced our ability to contain the current pandemic – leaving many hospitals without even the most basic personal protective equipment health workers need.

The undermining of care and care work, however, has a much longer history. Care has long been devalued due, in large part, to its association with women, the feminine and what have been seen as the 'unproductive' caring professions. Care work therefore remains consistently subject to less pay and social prestige, at least outside its expensively trained elite echelons. The dominant neoliberal model has merely drawn on these longer histories of devaluation, while twisting, reshaping and deepening inequality. After all, the archetypal neoliberal subject is the entrepreneurial individual whose only relationship to other people is competitive self-enhancement. And the dominant model of social organisation that has emerged is one of competition rather than co-operation. Neoliberalism, in other words, has neither an effective practice of, nor a vocabulary for, care. This has wrought devastating consequences.

The pandemic thus dramatically exposed the violence perpetrated by neoliberal markets, which has left most of us less able to *provide* care as well as less likely to *receive* it. We have, for a very long time, been rendered less capable of caring for people even in our most intimate spheres, while being energetically encouraged to restrict our care for strangers and distant others. No wonder right-wing and authoritarian populism has once again proved seductive. It has been easily fuelled, given the profound difficulties and unbearable collective anxieties of living in an uncaring world. Defensive self-interest thrives in conditions like these since, when our very sense of security and comfort is so fragile, it becomes harder to care for ourselves, let alone for others. In this way, care has been – and continues to be – overshadowed by totalitarian, nationalistic and authoritarian logics that rearticulate and reorient our caring inclinations towards 'people like us'. The spaces left for attending to difference or indeed developing more expansive forms of care have been rapidly diminishing. To appropriate a term famously used by Hannah Arendt, a systemic level of *banality* permeates our everyday carelessness. Hearing about catastrophes such as the vast numbers of drowned refugees, or the ever-expanding homelessness in our streets, has become routine. Most acts of 'not caring' happen unthinkingly. It is not that most of us actively enjoy seeing others left without the care they need, or that we share sadistic and destructive impulses. And yet we are failing to challenge the limits being placed upon our caring capacities, practices and imaginations.

What, we now ask, would happen if we were to begin instead to put care at the very centre of life?

In this manifesto, we argue that we are in urgent need of a politics that puts care front and centre. By care, however, we not only mean 'hands-on' care, or the work people do when directly looking after the physical and emotional needs of others – critical and urgent as this dimension of caring remains. 'Care' is also a social capacity and activity involving the nurturing of all that is necessary for the welfare and flourishing of life. Above all, to put care centre stage means recognising and embracing our *interdependencies*. In this manifesto we therefore use the term 'care' capaciously to embrace familial care, the hands-on care that workers carry out in care homes and hospitals and that teachers do in schools, and the everyday services provided by other essential workers. But it means as well the care of activists in constructing libraries of things, co-operative alternatives and solidarity economies, and the political policies that keep housing costs down, slash fossil fuel use and expand green spaces. Care is our individual and common ability to provide the political, social, material, and emotional conditions that allow the vast majority of people and living creatures on this planet to thrive – along with the planet itself.

Our approach in this manifesto is one that understands care as being active and necessary across every distinct scale of life. To begin with, the manifesto diagnoses the interconnected nature of the current reign of carelessness. It purposefully travels from the global dimensions that have produced the climate crisis and economies that put profit over people, through careless states and communities, to how the banality of carelessness ultimately affects our interpersonal intimacies. We then travel outward again, scaling up from the interpersonal to the planetary, in order to outline caring *alternatives* to our contemporary condition of carelessness. We use this structure, moving through these scales, because we want to show how our capacities to care are interdependent and cannot be realised in an uncaring world. Practices more conventionally understood as care, like parenting and nursing, in other words, cannot be properly carried out unless both caregivers and care receivers – indeed, all of us – are supported. This can only happen if care, as a capacity and a practice, is cultivated, shared and resourced on an egalitarian basis. It is not just 'women's work', and it should be neither exploited nor devalued. We thus begin by diagnosing the nature of the care crisis, showing in detail how and why social carelessness has come to structure and take hold of so many different dimensions of life. After this we offer solutions, sketching caring imaginaries which draw on past examples, present manifestations and future possibilities for forms of interconnected care. Rethinking these dependencies of care is pivotal for politics today if we hope to foster a politics of tomorrow.

Careless Worlds

We start with the most challenging scale: that of the global. We are all aware of the global nature of the coronavirus pandemic, and the lethally negligent lack of preparedness for it in so many countries, particularly the US and UK, despite recurrent warnings. Yet before Covid-19 grabbed all the headlines, every day had brought more stories about preventable disasters around the world: from refugees drowning in the Mediterranean Sea as they attempt to reach European shores, through the poisonous smog enveloping cities such as New Delhi, to the murder of unarmed black men and women in the US and the femicide of thousands of women (including significant numbers of trans women) killed annually in Latin America alone. The climate crisis is no longer imminent but unfolding before our eyes, with higher temperatures, deadly wildfires and flooding now commonplace. Extreme weather events are alarmingly frequent, wreaking havoc on communities, with the most vulnerable – whether poor black and brown communities in the US or low-lying countries in the Global South – invariably the hardest hit. All these phenomena are interrelated, for each is connected to the market-driven lack of care at every level of society.

Indeed, as neoliberal economic growth policies have become dominant in so many countries, the inherently careless practice of 'growing the economy' has taken priority over ensuring the well-being of citizens. Sprawling multinational corporations thrive under these conditions, free to pursue agendas that enrich the minority at the expense of the world. Oil giants, Big Pharma and high-tech firms like Google and Amazon have become more powerful and wealthier than many nation states, with precious little accountability to anyone. Moreover, these neoliberal policies and the monster corporations they create have intensified already existing inequalities both within countries and between the Global North and Global South, while simultaneously exacerbating environmental injustice and war, as well as facilitating the alarming rise of authoritarian regimes and ultra-nationalist rhetoric.

It is hardly surprising, then, that more right-wing governments have been voted into office in recent years, stoking the prevalent carelessness by building walls and tightening borders. While commodities continue to flow relatively unhindered, traditional borders are being strengthened to keep 'undesirable' people out. Such was Donald Trump's immediate reaction to the deadly coronavirus outbreak, once he'd reluctantly admitted that it *was* a global pandemic. This has happened in a context where the nature of borders had been dramatically changing already. Until recently, borders were the physical boundaries that contained nation states; today they have grown pervasive *within* nation states, their effects extending into ever more aspects of daily life. For instance, in the UK citizens are now encouraged to act like border guards and report anyone they suspect of being an undocumented migrant – an inevitably racialised and xenophobic practice. Moreover, 'grey zones' have developed between and within states, either as for-profit detention centres or in the form of refugee camps like the now dismantled 'jungle' in Calais, in which countless 'undesirables' (mostly poor and from the Global South) endure a purgatory of statelessness without legal rights or protections[1] – what Giorgio Agamben describes as 'bare life'.[2]

Such profound lack of care on a global scale has also created a world *that is itself in crisis*. Numerous economists and environmentalists have long argued that perpetual economic growth is completely incompatible with environmental limits and with preserving a habitable planet – from the Club of Rome's famous 1972 report on *The Limits of Growth* to more recent works, such as Ann Pettifor's *Case for the Green New Deal* and Kate Raworth's *Doughnut Economics*. A global neoliberal economy that places profit over people, and is dependent on the endless extraction and burning of fossil fuels, has caused environmental destruction on an unprecedented scale. The world, as Naomi Klein has recently written, is on fire.[3]

Carewashed Markets

Neoliberal capitalism is, then, an economic order concerned only with profits, growth and international competitiveness. It normalises endemic care deficits and abject failures to care at every level by positing them as necessary collateral damage on the road to market-oriented reforms and policies. While enabling certain modes of market-mediated and commoditised care, neoliberalism seriously undermines all forms of care and caring that do not serve its agenda of profit extraction for the few.

It is true that markets and marketplaces have always mediated some forms of care, from the Athenian agora to the petty traders and producers of the industrial era. Yet neoliberal capitalism is unique in putting forward an economic model of relentless markets alongside 'small government' in its bid to reduce all domains to market metrics. This kind of colonising market rationality is responsible for some of the very worst forms of carelessness in recent history. Economists including Thomas Piketty have vividly demonstrated how ever-rising income inequality is not an accident, but rather a key structural feature of neoliberal capitalism that is still increasing exponentially. Neoliberalism is uncaring by design.

Neoliberal market exchanges are primarily controlled by extremely powerful marketplace actors that are opaquely interconnected, globalised and largely reliant on governments for the creation of further 'freed' markets. Indeed, it is governments that have enabled the manoeuvres of large transnational corporations to reach unprecedented levels. At the same time, the supply chains that underlie these market exchanges are saturated with stories of extreme labour and planetary exploitation – from the Rana Plaza clothing factory collapse in Bangladesh to the staggeringly destructive oil extraction in Canada's tar sands. Invisible, undervalued, exploited care labour is everywhere, perhaps even heightened today with the advent of Covid-19: from the global care chains of our domestic workers to the hidden worker-carers who meticulously produce and circulate our essential goods.

Meanwhile, powerful business actors are promoting themselves as 'caring corporations' while actively undermining any kind of care offered outside their profit-making architecture. Thus, Wizz Air – a European low-cost airline – has as its advertising slogan 'Care More. Live More. Be More', reassuring its customers that 'Wizz cares' and therefore invests in carbon offsetting. Conspicuous by its absence is any admission that, above all, Wizz Air cares that we *carry on flying* but with less guilt, in order to make more money for its shareholders. Similarly, the Irish multinational clothes retailer Primark, synonymous with 'fast fashion', has in the past been notorious for its exploitation of child labour. But it has lately come up with a 'Primark cares' initiative, detailing how the company 'cares for people and planet', alongside a promotion of its new 'wellness products' (sweet-smelling candles and fluffy towels) in all its branches. In the UK, British Gas recently joined a campaign in favour of recognising unpaid care work, yet it still refuses to engage with mounting criticism over its lack of adequate care for the environment. Such forms of what we might term *carewashing* join a rich array of corporations trying to increase their legitimacy by presenting themselves as socially responsible 'citizens', while really contributing to inequality and ecological destruction. They go further by trying to capitalise on the very care crisis they have helped to create.

The proliferating expansion of platform-based markets for 'everyday care needs', from pet care and babysitters on care.com to the booming self-care and 'wellness' industry, is undermining our communal care resources and caring capacities by implanting market logics into traditional non-market realms, including those of health and education. Nation states themselves have facilitated many of the worst practices of global markets, allowing the evisceration of many of the basic forms of public provision, including healthcare, education, and housing, along with people's sense of responsibility for maintaining them.

Careless States

Since the 1980s the rulers of nation states – most notoriously Margaret Thatcher in the UK and Ronald Reagan in the US – have urged us to believe that care in all of its various manifestations is a matter for the individual, the supposed backbone of competitive markets and strong states. Such urgings are part of a spurious strand of self-discipline and a deceptive idea of the good and responsible citizen. The ideal citizen under neoliberalism is autonomous, entrepreneurial, and endlessly resilient, a self-sufficient figure whose active promotion helped to justify the dismantling of the welfare state and the unravelling of democratic institutions and civic engagement. This notion that care is up to the individual derives from the refusal to recognise our shared vulnerabilities and interconnectedness, creating a callous and uncaring climate for everyone, but particularly for those dependent on welfare, routinely accused of preferring 'worklessness and dependency'. Such views lay behind the recent implementation of the digitalised Universal Credit scheme for welfare payments in the UK, designed to whip almost all claimants into the workforce. Early on there were catastrophic consequences wherever it was implemented, inflicting extreme suffering on claimants while achieving nothing in savings.

As Danny Dorling shows in *Peak Inequality*, this wholesale lack of care and essential welfare support has been creating a calamitous environment in the UK.[4] The anguish exists at every level today, from rising infant mortality, through adolescent crime and increased physical and mental health problems, to family carers (especially of elderly parents or spouses) reporting constant strain due to benefit cuts and collapsing community resources. Its most dramatic manifestation of late is the conspicuously rising mortality rates among certain groups of the elderly, particularly working-class women, for the first time in a hundred years. Currently there are 1.5 million older people without the care they need in the UK, while suicide is on the increase and waiting times for mental health therapy have lengthened, despite more funding being available for limited, short-term therapy. While the coronavirus pandemic has forced the right-wing UK government to provide forms of social support only ever previously envisaged by the left, this profound legacy of inequality combined with deeply uneven provision has meant that the pandemic has hit the most neglected and disenfranchised constituencies hardest, particularly the elderly, women, BAME people, the poor and the disabled.[5] The picture is not so very different in other parts of the Global North.

At the same time, in the past few decades, welfare reform in the UK and in other European countries has been captured and monopolised by a very small group of global corporations that provide neither the 'value' nor the care they purport to. As Alan White revealed in his book, *Shadow State: Inside the Secret Companies That Run Britain,* there have been a succession of scandals and allegations of abuse involving large companies such as G4S, Serco, Capita, and Atos. Since these have won the bulk of contracts for running basic services including the NHS, the Ministry of Justice, asylum services, social care, disabilities and unemployment, they deal, often reprehensibly, with many of the most vulnerable people in our society.[6] Indeed, they have actively made more people extremely vulnerable: by, for example, working to expand prisons and the number of people incarcerated. With no effective government control over the giant companies it hires, this 'shadow state' takes advantage of the actual state. And the exponential growth of this unaccountable private sector has disastrous consequences, not only for our capacities to care – as we have seen in the UK's unreadiness for the spread of Covid-19 – but also for the possibility of democracy. It is, moreover, local communities which have been particularly hard hit by such practices, as national funds for local services dry up in many nation states, triggering the dismantling of some of the most essential forms of social provision and resources. This recent legacy of supporting the private sector at the expense of the public sector has been perversely notable during the pandemic, with larger corporations conspicuously the only constituency not being asked to take a financial hit by the more right-wing states. And as the pandemic continues, we are witnessing how this period has become the occasion for increased outsourcing in many countries, including the UK.

Uncaring Communities

Tragically, this deliberate rolling back of public welfare provision and resources, replaced by global corporate commodity chains, has generated profoundly unhealthy community contexts for care. Nowhere is this more apparent than in the social care sector itself. The corporate seizure of care homes from the public sector – a process enabled and imposed by government policies – has meant that the people being 'cared for' in their own communities are often neglected. The capacities of those employed to provide care are severely diminished through ongoing exploitation, understaffing, poor pay, time constraints, inadequate or non-existent job security and a lack of training and support.[7] Moreover, the loss of smaller and local providers, which were often firmly embedded in the community they served, further contributes to the unravelling of community ties.

The outsourcing of 'hands-on' care provision is, however, just one of the ways in which neoliberalism evacuates possibilities for maintaining community care. At the same time, we have also witnessed a massive contraction of public space, as corporations and private-sector actors have bought up and then privatised spaces that were once commonly owned and used by the people in the community. After the abolition of the Greater London Council (GLC) in 1986, for example, the large and handsome municipal County Hall and its surroundings, on the South Bank of the Thames, were sold off to a Japanese entertainment company.[8] The decimation of public spaces renders a sense of communal life increasingly difficult. There are fewer places for people to congregate, whether for relaxation and enjoyment, or to discuss issues of common concern or participate in collaborative projects. This heightens the competitive individualism that so often leads to loneliness and isolation, while having devastating repercussions for our ability to participate in democratic decision-making.

Fewer community resources, a culture that places profit over people, and a social and political landscape that incites us to focus on our individual selves has meant that cultivating community ties, which enhance democracy, has become ever harder. Such a care-less world creates fertile conditions for the growth of notoriously *uncaring* communities that base their sense of shared identity on exclusion and hatred – misogynist incel and white nationalist groups being paradigmatic examples. Moreover, careless communities focus on investing in policing and surveillance rather than in social provisions to promote human flourishing. And as carelessness takes hold in so many domains of life, and as community ties are profoundly weakened, the family is often encouraged to step in as society's preferred infrastructure of care.

Careless Kinships

The traditional nuclear family still provides the prototype for care and for contemporary notions of kinship, all stemming from the mythic ramifications of the first 'maternal bond'. This remains true even as queer people have been increasingly incorporated into the mainstream – on the condition that they reproduce the traditional nuclear-family model. Our circles of care have not broadened out but have, in fact, become painfully narrow.

These caring arrangements are unreliable and unjust. The nuclear family cannot be the assumed basic unit of care, nor can market outsourcing be the solution to the gender inequality of current care expectations or practices. In both cases, after all, women end up doing the lion's share of both unpaid and paid care work (two-thirds of paid and three-quarters of unpaid care work globally). Why should women have to do all this care work? And what if you don't have a family that can support you – what if your family has rejected you, or you have rejected them? What if you cannot afford to pay for privatised care services? At best, the consequences of this regime of care have often led to the neglect and isolation of those most in need of care, and at worst to needless sickness and death. The neoliberal insistence on only taking care of yourself and your closest kin also leads to a paranoid form of 'care for one's own' that has become one of the launch pads for the recent rise of hard-right populism across the globe. And this brings us full circle – from the global lack of care to the reliance on the traditional family – underscoring how the different scales we outline here are all intimately and inextricably related.

As we live through the ascendancy of far-right populism and the uncertainty of a post-pandemic world, the idea of care has been so diminished that it tends to mean care exclusively for and about 'people like us'. In what is a truly horrifying situation, the populist state actually strengthens itself the more it produces spectacles of indifference to the 'different'. Only a minority of us, apparently, feel upset when migrant infants are ripped away from their families; or when entire ecosystems burn to the ground as a result of climate change, or, as in Jair Bolsonaro's Brazil, are deliberately destroyed to make way for neoliberal capitalist ventures. One of the images that has come to define Trump's America is of US First Lady Melania Trump visiting a shelter that housed refugee children separated from their families, wearing a jacket with the words 'I Really Don't Care. Do U?' scrawled in big white letters. 'Really not caring' is presented by the right as a form of 'realism'; strong evidence of what we term the banality of carelessness. It also shows how crucial the question of dependency, and interdependency, is for our societies and our lives, at every single level, and the multiple destructions caused when these interdependencies are denied.

The Solution

How do we even begin to address the pervasiveness of carelessness? We suggest that we can do so by building on a wealth of examples of what we call 'care-in-practice', from the radical past to the recent present, when care has come to prominence as a vital force during the coronavirus emergency. In what follows, we offer a progressive vision of a world that takes the idea of care as its organising principle seriously, an idea that has been repudiated and disavowed for too long. This vision advances a model of 'universal care': the ideal of a society in which care is placed front and centre on every scale of life. Universal care means that care – in all its various manifestations – is our priority not only in the domestic sphere but in all spheres: from our kinship groups and communities to our states and planet. Prioritising and working towards a sense of universal care – and making this common sense – is necessary for the cultivation of a caring politics, fulfilling lives, and a sustainable world.

Achieving this vision of universal care is of course as challenging as it is pressing. It will involve avowing our mutual interdependencies and embracing the ubiquitous ambivalences at the heart of care and caregiving. It will mean ensuring that care is distributed in an egalitarian way – neither assumed to be unproductive and primarily women's work by nature, nor, when paid, carried out mostly by women who are poor, immigrant, or of colour. The goal is to ensure that the whole of society shares care's multiple joys and burdens. Across different scales of life, this vision translates into reimagining the limits of familial care to encompass more expansive or 'promiscuous' models of kinship; reclaiming forms of genuinely collective and communal life; adopting alternatives to capitalist markets and resisting the marketisation of care and care infrastructures; restoring, invigorating and radically deepening our welfare states; and, finally, mobilising and cultivating radical cosmopolitan conviviality, porous borders and Green New Deals at the transnational level.

1

Caring Politics

We begin by developing our radical vision of a caring world with our notion of a caring politics, in which care is both extensive and capacious, while traversing difference and distance. This is because care capacities and practices take different forms on each scale and in different dimensions of our lives. Our opening premise is that we must first and foremost recognise our mutual interdependencies and the intrinsic value of all living creatures. In doing so we draw on the insights of a host of feminist thinkers, including political theorists such as Joan Tronto who distinguishes between 'caring for', which includes the physical aspects of hands-on care, 'caring about', which describes our emotional investment in and attachment to others, and 'caring with', which describes how we mobilise politically in order to transform our world.[1] But these distinctions do not do justice to all care capacities and practices in their many diverse configurations and manifestations. Nor do they account for the paradoxes, ambivalences, and contradictions inherent in care and caretaking.

We therefore draw on a much wider range of thinkers and activists in order to sketch our understanding of care. This means moving back and forth from notions of proximate physical and emotional care, through theorising caring infrastructures and the nature of an overarching politics of care, to conceptualising care for strangers and distant others. To think of care as an organising principle on each and every scale of life, we argue that we must elaborate a feminist, queer, anti-racist and eco-socialist perspective, where care and care practices are understood as broadly as possible.

Dependency and Care

One of the great ironies surrounding care is that it is actually the rich who are most dependent on those they pay to service them in innumerable personal ways. Indeed, their status and wealth are partly signified by the number of people they rely upon to provide constant support and attention, from nannies, housemaids, cooks and butlers to gardeners and the panoply of workers outside their households who service their every need and desire. Yet this deep-rooted dependency remains veiled and denied so long as the very wealthy retain their full sense of agency, having the capacity to dominate or sack and replace those who care for them. However, the affluent project their own dependency onto those they pay to care for them, altering the meaning of dependency to make it synonymous with the economic subordination of those reliant on the paltry wages of caring work, while refusing to admit their own enduring need for care.

At the same time, in many countries those who should feel most *entitled* to care, such as the chronically ill, often report punitive humiliation when needing to make claims on the state, as though claimants must always be made to feel bad on some pretext or another.[2] We know from statistics released by the Department for Work and Pensions itself that in the UK, for instance, thousands have died after being declared fit for work. Even those needing short-term assistance while seeking work have been routinely subjected to intimidatory disciplinary regimes, with profoundly damaging psychological consequences which mental health workers have denounced. Dependence on care has been pathologised, rather than recognised as part of our human condition.

Why are these forms of interdependencies, and care itself, continually devalued and even pathologised?

One reason has to do with how autonomy and independence have historically been lionised in the Global North and gendered 'male'. Indeed, notions of unfettered male autonomy and independence remain symbolic of 'manhood', defined primarily in opposition to the 'soft', caring and dependent world of domesticity. Historically and to this day there is pressure on men to display a distinct and authoritative manhood, stoked in recent times by a wounded, sexist backlash to feminism. The dangers of this emaciated form of authoritative masculinity are only too apparent today. Awareness of its potential pathologies, seen in men's higher rates of suicide and of aggressive or irresponsible behaviour, has done little to displace these destructive masculine archetypes. It is no coincidence that the vast majority of mass shooters in the US are men – and white men at that – or that many have histories of violence directed at women. The problems stem, to a considerable degree, from their fears of displaying those figuratively feminine traits of frailty and weakness (and often manifest differently across class, age, race and battles for status within and between those occupying other hierarchies of power). In both past and present, men have frequently been punished for being 'less masculine', rather than encouraged to care and acknowledge their own dependencies.

Thus, care has historically been undervalued because it has been associated with the 'feminine' and with caretaking, which is understood to be women's work, tied in with the domestic sphere and women's centrality in reproduction. The conception of familial space and domesticity as a sphere of reproduction rather than production makes it all the easier for caring labour to be routinely exploited by the market, whether in the form of underpaid care workers or in its continuing reliance upon women's unpaid labour in the home. The assumption of women's caring nature also has a very long history, manifested in diverse ways over time. In the 1950s and 1960s, women were bombarded with images of the Happy Housewife and enveloped in the ideology of what Betty Friedan famously called 'the Feminine Mystique'. These views about women's natural caring capacities surrounded all those white Western women who became full-time housewives once they married – who themselves, perhaps, simply saw housekeeping as their expected role after marriage. One of the chief goals of second-wave feminism was not just to expose the high levels of loneliness, frustration and melancholy among many of these housebound women, but also to insist that raising children and domestic servicing are indeed forms of (often exhausting) work, no matter how willingly women might embark upon motherhood or perform the general caring and household labour.

However, times change, and sometimes rather fast. Today, there are almost as many women as men in the paid workforce in the Global North, often working ever longer hours to secure adequate financial resources for themselves and their families. As an increasing number of women have left the confines of the home and entered employment, we have seen the developing care crisis mutate and change shape. For many women, paid work has not only meant participation in the public sphere, it has also greatly increased the double burden they shoulder – the double burden of paid labour and unpaid domestic work which many working-class women have *always* carried. While statistics show that men overall are 'helping more' than previously in the home, the disparity in the amount of domestic labour carried out by men and women remains stark. Moreover, for women with slightly more resources, relieving the double burden has meant employing other women, predominantly poor, immigrant, and non-white women to shoulder the bulk of caring labour, particularly domestic servicing. This has in turn facilitated exploitative transnational care chains where women from the Global South migrate to the Global North to find jobs as care workers, often leaving their own children to be looked after by others. Racism thus combines with gender and global inequality to devalue the labour of care, ensuring the low pay and frequent exploitation of so many care workers, however essential and precious their caring labour is to their employers.

In Nancy Fraser's persuasive formulation, the traditional 'male breadwinner' model has thus been replaced with a more recent 'universal breadwinner' model, where both parents are encouraged or even compelled to *overwork* full-time. However, this does not have to be the solution. We fully support what Fraser calls the 'universal caregiver', where both parental care and equal opportunities in the paid workplace are valued.[3] But we also want to take this theory of care further, to promote the idea of 'universal care': the ideal of a society in which care is front and centre at every scale of life and in which we are all jointly responsible, for hands-on care work as well as the care work necessary for the maintenance of communities and the world itself. In practice, this does not mean that 'everyone has to do everything'. But it does mean cultivating and prioritising the social, institutional and political facilities that enable and enhance our capacities to care for each other and to restore and nurture rather than pillage the natural world. Prioritising and working towards a sense of universal care – and striving to make this common sense – is necessary for the cultivation of both a caring politics and fulfilling lives.

Ambivalences of Care

Of course, putting care front and centre at every scale of life will generate many challenges. The very concept 'care' overflows with paradoxes and ambivalence. Indeed, the distinctions between caring for, caring about, and caring with – which feminist scholars such as Tronto have developed – are useful, but do not account for the conflicting emotions that are inevitably part of different forms of care. Compared with similar complex, emotive terms such as courage, love or anger, the notion of care is rarely given due respect or attention. Even its mythic and etymological routes are tangled. The word care in English comes from the Old English *caru*, meaning care, concern, anxiety, sorrow, grief, trouble – its double meanings clearly on display. This reflects a reality where attending fully to the needs and vulnerabilities of any living thing, and thus confronting frailty, can be both challenging and exhausting. For instance, hands-on caring, however rewarding, also put us in contact with what may be the most daunting, even at times the most seemingly repellent or shameful, aspects of people's mortal, embodied selves. It is perhaps reassuring for many to pretend that those who perform the jobs that most disgust us, perhaps literally cleaning up our own or another's excrement, do so because 'that is all they are good for'. This is another reason why caring has been traditionally relegated to the domain of women, servants or others deemed inferior, while simultaneously serving to reinforce the notion of that inferiority – precisely because they are thought to be more suited to handling 'abject' flesh, the sign of our inescapable corporeal existence and hence of our mortality.

Sympathy and solicitude, like all other human emotions, always fluctuate, frequently at odds with other needs, desires, and affective states – such as the drive for personal gratification and recognition – or entangled with feelings of guilt or shame. The challenges of care, and in particular anxieties over whether it is being given well or even adequately, not to mention its devaluation, can easily fuel resentment or aggression in caring relationships, even in those often mythologised as exemplary. This is why feminists, such as Rozsika Parker in her classic text *Torn in Two: The Experience of Maternal Ambivalence* (1995) emphasised the importance of recognising the confused and contradictory emotions mothers have towards their children. Indeed, she sees recognising such caring ambivalence as itself energising and regenerative.[4]

Both positive and negative emotions inevitably entwine with both our care practices and our very capacities to care. It is because of the complexity and profound challenges of care, as capacity and practice, that we must provide and ensure the necessary social infrastructure that enables us to care for others, both proximate and distant. By this we mean, for example, ample resources and time. Parents and other carers facing the pressures of today's job markets routinely find they barely have time to provide for the essential needs of their dependants, let alone to pay heed to the situation of others in the outside world. Both more time and adequate material resources are essential to ground and facilitate mutually fulfilling and imaginative practices of care, from the domestic to the planetary level – and to foster the overall well-being of all creatures, human and non-human.

Ample resources and time in turn create the conditions that make a caring disposition towards the other, however distant, ever more possible. Only by ensuring this infrastructure can we work through at least some of the negative emotions that are inevitably tied up with care, whether in giving or receiving it. Far from public spending creating the pathologies of dependency, the reverse is true. Only with adequate and secure resources can anyone, however fragile and in need of specific assistance, develop and maintain whatever capabilities they have to enable some sense of autonomy, and escape from the pathologies of being rendered completely helpless and passive. This is well illustrated by disability rights activists who have argued for the *strategic* centrality of self-determination, or forms of 'independence', in which autonomy and control over their lives is key, precisely despite and because of their distinct needs:

> Independent Living does not mean that we want to do everything by ourselves, do not need anybody or like to live in isolation. Independent Living means that we demand the same choices and control in our everyday lives that our non-disabled brothers and sisters, neighbours and friends take for granted.[5]

We need to break the destructive linking of dependency with pathology and recognise that we are all formed, albeit in diverse and uneven ways, through and by our interdependencies.

Thus, in order to reimagine a genuinely caring politics, we must begin by recognising the myriad ways that our survival and our thriving are everywhere and always contingent on others. A caring politics must grasp both this interdependence and the ambivalence and anxiety it inevitably generates. Only once we acknowledge the challenges of our shared dependence, along with our irreducible differences, can we fully value the skills and resources necessary to promote the capabilities of everyone, whatever our distinct needs, whether as carers or cared for, noting the frequent reciprocity of these positions. Recognising our needs both to give and to receive care not only provides us with a sense of our common humanity, but enables us to confront our shared fears of human frailty, rather than project them onto those we label as 'dependent'.

Moreover, the practices of care that recognise the complexity of human interactions also enhance our ability to reimagine and participate more fully in democratic processes at all levels of society. After all, working with and through ambivalence and contradictory emotions is key to building democratic communities. Conversely, only by deepening participatory democracy, a core element in our broader vision of creating a more caring world, can we hope to properly work through the many ambivalences of care. And although we can never eliminate care's difficulties, we propose that we can mitigate them once we start building more caring kinships, communities, markets, states and worlds. Therefore, in what follows, we address all of these scales of life, step by step. As we show in later sections, this necessarily involves creating and defending the commons: collectively owned, socialised forms of provision, space and infrastructure. However, since our current regimes of care attempt to silo care on the scale of kinship as much as possible, our critique of these regimes and our imagining of what should replace them starts with the family.

2

Caring Kinships

Only by multiplying our circles of care – in the first instance, by expanding our notion of kinship – will we achieve the psychic infrastructures necessary to build a caring society that has universal care as its ideal. In this chapter, by drawing on a range of caring arrangements common in other periods or places and based on alternative kinship structures, we put forward a new ethics of 'promiscuous care' that would enable us to *multiply* the numbers of people we can care for, about and with, thus permitting us to *experiment* with the ways that we care.

Alternative Caring Kinships

We need not look far to find cultures where caring kinships have been arranged differently. Whether by necessity or design, care beyond the nuclear family has been acceptable to different degrees in different societies for centuries, some examples more radical than others.

Take 'mothering', still upheld in our culture as the archetypal caring relationship, but one whose practices are so rigidly idealised that they may often burden even those women who desire the role and have the resources to perform it. But mothering has been imagined differently. In African American communities, where racism has made resources scarce and life more precarious, black women have long reimagined what mothering might look like, dividing childcare between 'blood mothers' and 'other-mothers'. A blood mother is a child's biological mother, whereas other-mothers are the network of women a biological mother can rely on when she is not available to care for her child. This model of kinship, informed by West African traditions, adopted new forms when black women became the primary carers of white children instead of their own, whether as slaves or as exploited domestic labourers. As a category, other-mothers would include family members – grandmothers, sisters and cousins – but, importantly, it would also include neighbours and friends. This expanded notion of kinship eased the burden of care for an already overburdened social group and spread the joys as well as the challenges of caring to other women in the community.[1]

Closely related were the experiments in childcare that took place as part of second-wave feminism in the 1970s. The burden of childcare, its devaluation as a practice, and the way it worked to preclude women from participating in public life were all key objects of feminist struggle during this time. Second-wavers proposed different solutions. Some championed collective living arrangements (with and without men) in which all domestic labour, including childcare, was shared equally, so that all members could engage in the burdens and pleasure of care work as well as having a life outside the domestic realm. Others argued for well-resourced maternity leave and differing childcare arrangements, including co-operative nurseries and crèches (where men of the left also worked at times).

A term we might use to describe these collective childcare arrangements is 'families of choice'.[2] This term was developed primarily in relation to LGBT political movements contemporary with second-wave feminism. It originally referred not so much to childcare as to relationships outside the biological family, which LGBT folk felt were the most significant to them. Families of choice emerged because non-normative sex or gender expressions could (and still can) cause a person to be rejected by their biological family. As a result, LGBT people often moved to 'gay neighbourhoods' within cities and forged family like relationships with friends and lovers who fulfilled their caring needs. This was often out of necessity, but it was also advocated as part of the radical politics of gay liberation that sought to expand affective relations of care and intimacy beyond those sanctioned by and through heteronormativity.

Indeed, as societies 'de-traditionalised' in the late twentieth century, partly as a result of these social movements, the alternative kinship structures they encouraged started to migrate into the lives of people who did not necessarily consider themselves radical. In empirical work carried out by sociologist Sasha Roseneil with Shelley Budgeon in the early 2000s, they discovered that it was very often friends, rather than relatives or partners, who were the primary carers of people in different parts of the UK. Friends cohabited, looked after each other's children and performed palliative care for the sick and the dying. The problem was, and remains, that there was not enough state recognition of these friendships to furnish them with either the decision-making powers or the resources necessary to care as well as they would have wished, making them less secure over the long term. Entirely in keeping with the spirit of this manifesto, Roseneil argues at the end of her study that 'the friend' could easily replace 'the mother' as the archetypal figure in our caring imaginaries, and that 'networks and flows of intimacy and care' should replace the family as the prime relational unit.[3]

There is surely no greater illustration of the failures of both neoliberalism and hetero-patriarchal kinship in providing adequate infrastructures of care than the AIDS crisis of the 1980s and '90s, a crisis which still persists among African Americans and in large parts of Africa. The market was incapable of responding to the speed and scale at which HIV/AIDS spread through different communities during the early years of the outbreak. And when it came to gay men and trans women – two of the largest demographics affected at the time – sufferers were frequently let down by their biological families too.

Building on the community models of the Black Panthers, and feminist and gay liberation healthcare initiatives from the 1970s, community organisations of varying sizes and political stripes emerged to fill the gaps. In the US and the UK groups like ACT UP, Gay Men Fighting AIDS, Buddies and the Terrence Higgins Trust drew together gay men, lesbians, second-wave feminists, and people of colour to demand that the government, Big Pharma and the general public wake up and care about the marginalised populations being decimated by the disease, while also developing initiatives that could provide care for them. The scale of the crisis meant that these bottom-up efforts could only ever be partially successful. Nevertheless, they sketched out an important model for looking after others, and offered a vivid example that can help transform our notions of what constitutes caring kinship. We might call this kind of care network 'strangers like me': forms of care carried out by strangers whose lives resemble our own.

The care for 'strangers like me' has taken on an intriguing twist in our digital times. The digital sociologist Paul Byron has researched the often life-saving forms of care unfolding among trans people on the social media platform, Tumblr. Despite the advances made by LGBT+ movements over the past fifty years, trans folk remain among the most marginalised of social groups. They are at greater risk of violence, more likely to commit suicide, and are severely under-resourced when it comes to their care needs. Byron's work shows how Tumblr constitutes an ideal space for this community to come together and provide care for each other.[4] Unlike other platforms, Tumblr does not require users to identify themselves on their profile, allowing them to visit the platform anonymously. This anonymity is vital for a group who either may not have fully come to terms with their gender identity, or for whom expressing it publicly could be life-threatening. As a result, Tumblr has become a site where trans people from around the world share information, advice and emotional support. It offers a space of organisation, belonging and care. This phenomenon helps us think about the significant place of the digital in relation to care (beyond the exploitative models of platforms like care.com, which profits from inefficiently attempting to match gig-economy care workers with those in need of care), with its ability to encompass care towards people whom we do not know and cannot even see.

Caring across Difference

Useful as they are in helping us think about care beyond the nuclear family, the alternative kinship structures that we have just outlined rely on a notion of hands-on care (care for) and are based on some degree of sameness – even if it is the sameness of a shared illness or worldview. The more challenging issue when it comes to imagining new models of care is that of caring across difference – whichever way 'difference' is constructed in a particular time and space.

Parallel to other theorists of subjective interdependency, the philosopher Emmanuel Levinas held that because the self is constituted only through its relationship to the other, we are ethically compelled to that other's care. Drawing on this idea and on cultures of hospitality, the French philosopher Jacques Derrida advocated an ethics of limitless hospitality to 'the stranger'. Echoes of the Derridean model of hospitality are found in some unlikely places, not least in the various improvised welcome centres formed in response to the European refugee crisis. In City Plaza, for instance – a hotel in the centre of Athens that was squatted from April 2016 to July 2019 – activists and residents insisted that the project was about more than just 'taking care' of the 400 people living there. Rather, it was often described as an 'alternative family' aiming to make City Plaza 'home' to a shifting mix of mostly Syrian refugees (but also Eritreans, Ghanaians, Iranians, Somalis) and many European 'solidarians'.

Stretching the concept of caring kinship, perhaps to its very limit, is the care extended by military medics to enemy combatants wounded on the battlefield. In a sense there is no greater challenge to our caring imaginaries than to tend to people who are trying to kill 'people like us'. Nevertheless, it is a practice of care enshrined in the Hippocratic Oath, as well as international law, and undergirded by the ethical frameworks of many major religions. It shows that you do not have to look too far outside the mainstream to find a multiplicity of extant caring practices that can provoke us into thinking about care in more expansive terms, beyond the shrivelled forms that prevail today.

What about kinship in relation to the 'non-human' – animals and the environment? Historian Nick Estes addresses this question in his work on the politics of Standing Rock, in which he argues that there is a capaciousness to Native American conceptions of kinship 'that goes beyond the human'. Kinship is not tied only to blood or family but extends to the land, water, and the animals on whom we depend for livelihood. For the Water Protectors at Standing Rock, resistance to the Dakota Pipeline was precisely about protecting a *relative*, Mni Sose (the Missouri River). Moreover, for the Dakota, kinship is also a process: 'making kin is to make people into familiars in order to relate.'[5] This conception of kinship derives from Indigenous beliefs about the centrality of cultivating just relations with human and non-human relatives and with the earth. Such relationships are fundamental to developing a politics of care, from the most intimate kinships to the planetary scale.

Promiscuous Care

We have surveyed care at the scale of kinship because, within the current arrangements, it is all too often inadequate, unreliable and unjust. If care is to become the basis of a better society and world, we need to change our contemporary hierarchies of care in the direction of radical egalitarianism. All forms of care between all categories of human and non-human should be valued, recognised and resourced equally, according to their needs or ongoing sustainability. This is what we call an ethics of promiscuous care.

We base this ethics of promiscuous care on AIDS activist theory from the 1980s and 1990s, specifically the essay 'How to Have Promiscuity in an Epidemic', by the academic and ACT UP activist, Douglas Crimp.

This essay was a response to the idea, advanced not only in the media but also by gay leaders, that one origin of the AIDS epidemic lay in the sexual promiscuity of gay men. Crimp retorted that what the so-called promiscuity of post-Stonewall sexual cultures actually meant for the epidemic was that gay men 'multiplied' 'experimental' sexual practices, beyond the penetrative sex that was one of the more common routes of HIV transmission. He writes that some gay leaders 'insist that our promiscuity will destroy us when in fact it is our promiscuity that will save us'.[6] Here Crimp uses the concept not in the sense of 'casual' or 'indifferent', but in that of multiplying and experimenting with the ways gay men were intimate with and cared for each other. These experimental intimacies ultimately served as the basis for the safer sex initiatives, developed by groups like ACT UP, that went on to save countless lives.

In the same spirit, we must also *care* promiscuously. In advocating for promiscuous care, we do not mean caring casually or indifferently. It is neoliberal capitalist care that remains detached, both casual and indifferent, with disastrous consequences. For us, promiscuous care is an ethics that proliferates outwards to redefine caring relations from the most intimate to the most distant. It means caring *more* and in ways that remain experimental and extensive by current standards. We have relied upon 'the market' and 'the family' to provide too many of our caring needs for too long. We need to create a more capacious notion of care.

'Promiscuous' also means 'indiscriminate', and we argue that we must not discriminate when we care. Building on historic formations of 'alternative' caregiving practices, we must expand our caring imaginaries further still: anyone can potentially care for, about and with anyone. The caring state, in recognising this, would furnish both carer and cared for with the legal, social and cultural recognition and the resources they need. This, in turn, will enhance our abilities to cultivate an orientation towards the other – whether distant or proximate – that is caring. The question of resources is critical here. Looking at promiscuous care from another angle: if the neoliberal defunding and undermining of care has led to paranoid and chauvinist caring imaginaries – looking after 'our own' – adequate resources, time and labour would make people feel secure enough to care for, about and with strangers as much as kin.

Of course, promiscuous care does not mean that we care only fleetingly for strangers or they only care fleetingly for us. It does, however, recognise that care can be carried out by people with a wide range of kinship connections to us. Sometimes care is best carried out by strangers, or indeed can *only* be carried out by strangers. Just look at the mutual aid groups that have sprung up during the Covid-19 pandemic. Where would these frail and isolated people be, were it not for the anonymous care given to them by strangers who risked their own infection by delivering essential goods and medicines? Of course, had the NHS not been so eviscerated by a decade of Tory-administered austerity, the state might have been able to provide this care without calling on groups of self-organised volunteers. Or perhaps a more caring state would have the mechanisms in place to fund and support these self-organised volunteers. In our vision we believe all care work should be properly resourced and democratically organised, not left to the free labour of strangers. And, of course, properly resourced care for and by a stranger begins to make that stranger more familiar, reinforcing the bonds of promiscuous care.

Promiscuous care must also recognise that history, culture and habit make some forms of care more likely than others – including parental care – and that the time, resources and wider infrastructures must be made available by the state and communities to support them, as we lay out later. But nothing is immutable. Sometimes a mother cannot look after her child, or at least not adequately, for a range of different reasons, and promiscuous care would proliferate the types of care that are available to both child and mother (since the mother needs caretaking too). Promiscuous care recognises that not all women *want* to be mothers, whether they *can* be or not; and that caring for children who are not your own, caring for the community and caring for the environment are equally valuable tasks that must be adequately resourced and appreciated. Promiscuous care argues that caring for migrants and refugees should carry the same significance that our culture places on caring for our own, and urges us to care about the fate of those children forcibly separated from their families at the US border and placed in detention centres, as if they were kin. It recognises that we all have the capacity to care, not just mothers and not just women, and that all our lives are improved when we care and are cared for, and when we care together. There is no category of human, or indeed non-human, to whom this does not apply.

To encourage promiscuous care means building institutions that are capacious and agile enough to recognise and resource wider forms of care at the level of kinship. But promiscuous care should also inform every scale of social life: not just our families but our communities, markets, states, and our transnational relationships with human and non-human life as well. In this sense it connects to what we called 'universal care' in the introductory chapter. In the next, we consider how universal and promiscuous care can also be realised at the level of community.

3

Caring Communities

Over the past few decades, many of us have experienced living in an accelerating social system of *organised loneliness*. We have been encouraged to feel and act like hyper-individualised, competitive subjects who primarily look out for ourselves. But in order to really thrive we need caring communities. We need localised environments in which we can flourish: in which we can support each other and generate networks of belonging. We need conditions that enable us to act collaboratively to create communities that both support our abilities and nurture our interdependencies.

This is because issues of care are not just bound up with the intimacy of very close relationships, such as family and kinship. They also take shape in the environments we inhabit and move through – in local communities, neighbourhoods, libraries, schools and parks, in our social networks, and the groups we belong to.

But how do we create the kind of caring communities that make our lives better, happier, and even, in some cases, possible? What kind of infrastructures are necessary to create communities that care?

We argue that there are four core features to the creation of caring communities: mutual support, public space, shared resources and local democracy. First, communities based on caregiving and caretaking provide members with a range of *mutual support*, from neighbourliness to, for instance, coronavirus mutual aid groups. As we showed in the previous chapter, such forms of support are often spontaneous and generated from down to up, but they also require structural support to be consistent and survive over time. Second, caring communities need *public space*: space that is co-owned by everyone, is held *in common* and is not commandeered by private interests.[1] Expanding our common public space means reversing the neoliberal compulsion to privatise everything. Third, communities that care prioritise the sharing of resources – both material resources, such as tools, and 'immaterial' ones such as online information – *between* and *among* people, rather than the hoarding of resources by the few, or the planned obsolescence of disposable, single-use objects. Fourth, caring communities are democratic. They must extend localised engagement and governance through radical municipalism and co-operatives, and rebuild the public sector through expanding and 'insourcing' its caring and welfare activities, rather than the outsourcing that accompanies privatisation. We show how these features can and do work by referring to some tangible examples, past and present. Caring communities need to be strengthened, pluralised and diversified by building up these four features, which, brought together, form what we call a 'sharing infrastructure' at community level.

Mutual Support

Communities based on caregiving and caretaking provide each other with forms of mutual support. This is palpable in the idea of being a good neighbour, looking out for those who live nearby. Whether it involves checking in on those who are ill, running errands, keeping a spare set of keys, watering plants or feeding pets, 'neighbourliness' is a powerful and widely practised informal mode of localised and mutual community care. The development of local mutual aid groups in Europe and elsewhere during the Covid-19 pandemic has been an excellent example of how such neighbourly support networks can expand to provide what we term 'promiscuous care'.[2] Caring for a wide range of people by offering forms of support beyond immediate kinship networks is one hallmark of a caring community.

At the same time, localised and neighbourly forms of mutual support also have the potential to help communities become more egalitarian, or less unequal and unjust. For instance, many of the informal shared childcare groups created by the Women's Liberation Movement in the 1970s around the Western world enabled women to spend time on other things than childcare, and hence to play a greater role in the public sphere alongside men.[3]

To extend these forms of localised mutual practice on a more expansive and consistent level, they need scaling up and structural support. Again, childcare is a good example, as many of those 1970s informal crèches grew into permanent day-care centres. Other important instances of mutual aid becoming extended and formalised are community co-operatives – collectively owned forms of provision that share their assets. These have multiple manifestations across different spheres, from housing to food, in a wide range of periods and countries. They include the Rochdale Pioneers of mid-nineteenth-century northern England: tradesmen who joined forces to sell wares at cost price, something they could not otherwise afford during the Industrial Revolution. We hear their echoes today in co-operative credit unions in the US and elsewhere, allowing people to save and borrow more easily while benefitting their communities, not the rich. They include the Mondragon federation of co-operatives in the Basque country of Spain, which emerged in the 1950s as a collective response to the fascist regime of General Franco. Another historical example is the Tredegar Workmen's Medical Aid Society, which brought together financial resources from across its Welsh community to provide medical care for all – a model later massively scaled up to create the NHS. The strength and historical popularity of the co-operative form is often underplayed, but it is a potent and crucial instance of mutual support in communities and, as we will see, of constructing caring economies.

Caring communities, then, need to facilitate diverse forms of *mutual support*. Some of these practices will inevitably remain informal. Those that directly affect social egalitarianism, life chances and public health need structural support, especially from local and national government. Moreover, to create the conditions for such mutual forms of caring to genuinely flourish and expand, communities also need public space.

Space to Care

Public spaces are crucial for building caring communities because they are egalitarian and accessible to all, and can foster conviviality, interconnections and the emergence of communal life. We must create, take back and demand more public space.

The Greater London Council (GLC) between 1981 and 1986 was exemplary in showing how a municipal council could provide shared spaces for economic, social and cultural initiatives. Its efforts to expand and reinvigorate democratic cultural life were renowned for their radicalism, both in prioritising people who had traditionally been marginalised by UK arts policy (women, people of colour, gay and disabled people), and in making such events *popular*. It trimmed the subsidised funding for traditionally 'high culture' venues, like the Royal Opera House, and instead put money into community arts. Its initiatives ranged from supporting large, free music festivals to subsidising local arts centres, community radio and feminist magazines such as *Spare Rib* and organisations such as Southall Black Sisters. In this way, GLC policies helped to democratise intellectual and cultural activity across London.[4]

Crucially, the GLC made its larger sites more accessible, thereby extending the public commons. Hitherto, London's vast arts complex, the Southbank Centre, had been the exclusive and pricey preserve of the upper and upper middle classes, until the GLC created a new 'open foyer' policy in its flagship building, the Royal Festival Hall. This allowed anyone, with or without a ticket, to enter and hang out. Today it is still one of the relatively few covered public places in the British capital, besides libraries, churches and museums, where it's possible to spend time without spending money – which makes it a haven for many, especially those with young children.[5] Reclaiming and extending 'public place-making', then, enables us to build communities that care.

Similarly, our architectural and environmental infrastructures also need to prioritise sharing. The reorganisation of space can foster the cultivation of genuinely collectivist, rather than atomised, logics – and improve our health and our surroundings in the process. Publicly owned parks, which need protecting and expanding, and should include areas where local communities can grow things, give people access to nature, to exercise, and to spaces in which to encounter 'others' in the everyday. Such encounters extend beyond the human. Green spaces are often carved up into individual gardens, while the fully fenced, totally sealed-off garden stops the movement of wildlife. Gardens which are shared, either fully or partially, enable us to travel through and socialise, via communal walks and 'playways': they nurture more community care and more life-in-common on every level.

This interconnection is also true of the built environment. We need policies enabling co-operative housing, collective housing and rent caps, as well as imaginative architects and planners who can facilitate forms of connective care and infrastructural sharing. This means prioritising green spaces and public transport over cars and roads, and creating the resources to cultivate caring communities based on a notion of the commons: owning and sharing together. Put differently, we need the 'right to the city', a slogan widely used to reclaim cities as co-produced spaces to be extended everywhere, for everyone – as well as the right to the suburbs and the countryside.

Communities, then, need a wide range of outdoor and indoor, online and offline public zones in order to flourish. These include spaces for those with specific needs, such as care homes, housing co-ops, youth clubs, hospitals, schools and nurseries, as well as those more general forms of provision for health and recreation, such as parks, community centres, libraries, galleries, and swimming pools. Creating communities that can care means amplifying the spaces that are public, that are held in common, that are shared and co-operative, rather than those designed for or hijacked in the interests of private capital. To do this is to create what we term a *sharing infrastructure*, which involves mutual support and public community space. It also involves sharing community resources.

Sharing Stuff

Local libraries remain one of the most powerful examples of non-commodified local space and resource-sharing. They enable us to read widely, and can also work as community hubs, providing internet access and meeting space for people to learn and connect. Crucially, libraries are places where there's no need to buy multiple copies of individual things or to contribute to overconsumption, because books can be *shared*. Sharing material and immaterial resources is a path to both environmental sustainability and community collaboration. But these facilities require time, infrastructure and support in order to function effectively, to be sustainable, and to expand, in contrast to the drastic cuts they have been subject to.[6] Libraries can be experimental community spaces for the twenty-first century that can provide inventive activities and resources for local communities. But they should also have funded staff and actual books. We need both community spaces *and* shared resources.

The powerful community model of local libraries deserves to be both cherished and developed. Yet we can also move beyond books, to develop more 'libraries of things' and other forms of reuse and recirculation. In an era of imminent climate catastrophe, it is obscenely wasteful for people to buy hardware they might use only a few times a year, whether we are talking about power drills, expensive children's toys or waffle makers. It's possible to refuse the disastrous capitalist system of planned obsolescence and share objects within communities. As a result we would limit carbon emissions, save money, and develop our capacities to care not only for animate but also inanimate things.

Several 'libraries of things' already exist. In Athens, for instance, anti-consumerist collectives such as Skoros have been renting former retail premises and running them entirely on a volunteer basis for over ten years, so that anyone can borrow, gift and/or take clothes, books, toys, kitchenware and other items, as well as participate in various DIY workshops for free.[7] In the US, there are several successful tool libraries dating back to the 1970s, such as Rebuilding Together Central Ohio's and Seattle's Phinney Neighborhood Association tool libraries; and there is a repository of borrowable kitchenware in Oregon. In various London neighbourhoods, examples include a toy library, a local facility lending equipment from gardening tools and popcorn makers to gazebos, and a mobile 'Share Shed'. And today there is a new wave of interest in 'libraries of things', as well as in gifting bazaars, clothes swaps (or 'swishing'), freecycling and social media swap sites, alternative currency systems, and reuse workshops, indicating the enormous resourcefulness and creativity of local communities. These need to become embedded as part of the community, becoming the new normal, rather than a series of ad-hoc solutions.

We can also share *immaterial* resources to collectivise our skills and knowledge. One way is by creative use of 'time banks', which enable people to swap the time they spend on doing activities or jobs for each other, or via skillshare sessions, alongside the rich tradition of local activity clubs and DIY workshops. Just as we can share physical resources, so too do we need equal access to online resources. These should be maintained through digital infrastructures that we co-own: thus, instead of platform capitalism there would be platform co-operativism.[8] As the coronavirus crisis has made painfully clear – and as the Labour Party proposed in its 2020 manifesto – broadband should be counted as an essential service and collectively owned. Sharing resources facilitates working and being together; without equal access, people become excluded and isolated. So, while we clearly need communities in order to share, what is perhaps less obvious is that sharing, in turn, helps to create community.

Caring Communities Are Democratic Communities

There are profound interconnections, then, between mutual support, public space, sharing resources and community life. Reinforcing all these areas makes localised forms of democracy both more possible and more obviously important. But how do we scale them up?

Over the last few years, one inspiring example is how Preston council in north-west England dealt with having its budget slashed by encouraging localism and workers' co-operatives.[9] It switched its public sector priorities from spending money on corporate contractors hundreds of miles away to investing in local providers and worker-owned co-operatives. The hugely successful Preston Model echoes Ohio's Cleveland Model, in which the state actively intervened to build the capacity of local co-operatives. At a time when many baby-boomer business owners were retiring, the Cleveland Model encouraged existing companies to be sold to their workers through a combination of training and financial support.[10] These collective projects empower local workers and give them a say over what happens in their communities. Such structural support for community wealth-building and control over production, as well as democratic ownership and governance, is what care for and by communities must involve.

Both the Cleveland and Preston models, like Cooperation Jackson in the US and Barcelona en Comú (Barcelona in Common), are examples of what has been called 'the new municipalism' or 'remunicipalism'. Municipalism is the practice of self-government by an area, town or city. While there are political complexities to these forms, the key feature of the new municipalism is that it breaks with the neoliberal system of siphoning off public money to feed remote multinational corporations.[11]

The new muncipalism mobilises local 'community wealth-building' to counteract the exploitation of global capitalist commodity chains. They can also enable what Keir Milburn and Bertie Russell describe as 'public–commons partnerships', in which co-operative institutions link up with public services and local citizens with an active stake in their organisation.[12] In its leftist and co-operative form, rather than its authoritarian, right-wing manifestation as practised by Viktor Orbán in Hungary, municipalism offers a way forward for communities to care democratically. This is what Emma Dowling calls 'municipal care' – the opposite of the temporary 'care fixes' engineered by so-called compassionate capitalism.[13]

A crucial dimension of municipal, democratic care would come from its *insourcing*, once public provision is brought back 'in-house'. With jobs returning to the public sector, workers gain job security, living wages and pensions, as well as sick and holiday pay. Insourcing is thus an act of caring for workers that also puts them into a position where *they can care more*. The failure of the privatised care home system, which has seen, in Bev Skeggs's words, 'the state being treated like an ATM machine' while workers and clients suffer, has been highlighted by the coronavirus crisis. Thousands of people have died in care homes, staff have been left with inadequate or no protective equipment, and, most tragically, many old people were in the early days of the pandemic largely abandoned, their deaths from the coronavirus not even recorded. Care homes need to be run on a not-for-profit basis, by the local authority wherever possible. Positive examples here include the care homes being brought back into the public sector in British Columbia, Canada; and the Buurtzorg social care co-operative in the Netherlands, which works with the needs of the client, is rated extremely highly by users and employees, and moreover saves 40 per cent in costs to the national healthcare system by prioritising quality and need over profit.[14]

Such municipal projects are creating radically democratic social ecologies of care at the community level. Institutional forms and networks which can truly generate care are those that are based not on private profit but on socialised forms of provision which involve users in their planning and production. Providing the necessary sharing infrastructure, giving communities a greater role in planning their locality and its services, remaking the relations between the state and local levels to deepen collaborative decision-making (or 'co-production') are key for creating communities with the capacity to care. Crucially, as well, in the process they are doing something else: they are deepening democracy.

Caring in Common

As we have shown, the local communities we traverse need to be built upon the desire for mutual thriving. This means empowering communities by resourcing public space, facilitating mutual aid through structured forms of useful communal resources, and building the ability to engage meaningfully with decisions as to how communities are run. The possibilities for democratic involvement need to be expanded across an array of spheres and zones, whether in local government, political formations, public services, schools, unions or neighbourhood assemblies, a theme we will return to later.

Communities can, of course, be romanticised. We can all think of examples of 'non-care' in the community. From 'care homes' not worthy of the name, to the negative solidarity of mutual suspicion and scapegoating, the idea of care can be used to push controlling and reactionary agendas. To be clear, what 'caring communities' does *not* mean is using people's spare time to plug the caring gaps left wide open by neoliberalism. It means ending neoliberalism in order to expand people's capacities to care. To be truly democratic will involve forms of municipal care that put an end to corporate abuse, generate co-operatives and replace outsourcing with insourcing. Then, instead of corporate control over increasingly atomised, impoverished, endangered and divided communities, we can create co-operative communities: communities that are coproduced, that enable us to connect, to deliberate and to debate, to find joy and to flourish, and to support each other's needs amidst the complexities of our mutual dependencies.

4

Caring States

The state is a critical arena if we are to create any sort of universal care. States must cease to be places where the interests of corporate-driven patterns of economic growth predominate, as these routinely rest upon deepening inequality, including embedded ethno-nationalism. Instead, their first and ultimate responsibility should be to build and maintain their own sustainable infrastructures of care. This means turning the current priorities of most nation states on their head.

A caring state is one in which notions of belonging are based on a recognition of our mutual interdependencies, rather than on ethno-cultural identity and racialised borders defended in the name of national security. It is one in which the provision for all of our basic needs is assured while, at the same time, it caters to the health of the environment and deepens participatory democracy at every level. The caring state is only successful inasmuch as it nurtures every human being and other living creatures within its bounds. And while no state can ever completely eliminate human aggression, relations of domination, or natural and human-made disasters, a caring state provides the conditions in which the vast majority of people can, nevertheless, not only survive but thrive.

First and foremost, a caring state must resource all the structures that facilitate the well-being and foster the capabilities or sustainability of all human and non-human life within its domain. For this to happen, we must transform the way belonging and citizenship operate within current state borders. For many countries, such as the US, this will often mean taking the lead from the struggles of Indigenous and First Nations People. In line with Canada's *Leap Manifesto*, we argue that there must not only be recognition of past atrocities but also a reckoning with and some form of reparation for them, whether genocide, slavery and/or dispossession. This will, of necessity, entail a process of decolonisation and the reclamation of stolen lands as well as stolen lives. It will also include reassessing how histories of imperialism and inequality are narrated in public heritage spaces and educational institutions. Only by confronting the past and prioritising the needs of those who have been most marginalised, violated and negated by uncaring nation states will we be able to move forward into a juster future and cultivate a radically different way of relating to others and the world itself.

States, in short, need urgently to build a care infrastructure based upon a recognition of our profound interdependencies and vulnerabilities, while putting the necessary material, social, and cultural conditions in place for the mutual thriving of all. Can this be done? It can, but first we must rethink the earlier, Keynesian welfare model.

The Welfare State and Its Discontents

We often hear resentment expressed towards the older generation of so-called baby boomers, the 'lucky generation'. It was this generation that largely benefited from the expanding post-war welfare state, following the New Deal in the US and William Beveridge's promise, in his famous 1942 Report, to provide care and support for everybody 'from cradle to grave'. Influenced by Keynesian economics, with its warning that markets could not be relied upon to regulate themselves, the new post-war consensus generated widespread support for far-reaching extension of social services and state resources. This happened despite the fact that many European governments were near bankrupt as a result of the war. During this period, in many countries in the Global North, the state was understood to be responsible for facilitating the well-being of its citizens and for improving social infrastructures, while helping to ensure decent lives for all – whatever the shortcomings in practice, particularly in relation to racialised subjects and the realities (and eventual legacies) of colonialism. By the 1950s, for instance, 20 per cent of the British economy was publicly owned, including most essential services such as transport, energy and other key industries, and by 1979 almost half the British population lived in council housing, with the gap between the richest and poorest lower than ever before.

Similar policies were pursued across much of the Western world, supported by higher levels of progressive taxation. In the UK, the pioneer of British social policy, Richard Titmuss, insisted on the importance of universal benefits, conceived as entitlements, to ensure all citizens had an equal interest in the state, while judging gross inequalities to be both 'morally wrong and corrosive of a healthy society'. In popular radio broadcasts, the British psychoanalyst D. W. Winnicott highlighted the fact of human dependency, stressing the essential importance of 'holding environments' for the child, which fed into ideas about the significance of caring welfare states through support for mothers and the provision of decent homes and welfare services.[1]

Rethinking the Keynesian Welfare State

A state organised around care would adopt many of the initial post-1945 welfare promises, while working to eliminate the inherently sexist, racist, hierarchical premises and manifestations of that time, and combating the anti-immigrant xenophobia still so evident today. A caring state will always begin by valuing caretaking over profit-making, and champion caretaking as a highly valued end in itself.

Our vision of a caring state is one in which each life is understood to have intrinsic value and where belonging is not defined over and against a racialised or subordinated other. The caring state ensures high-quality and flexible care that is predominantly free at the point of use during all stages of life, from infancy to old age. It provides as well as ensures affordable housing and shared public and cultural spaces for all, along with high-quality public schooling, vocational training, university education and healthcare. A caring state recognises that its infrastructure as well as its day-to-day functioning depend on a myriad of skills and competencies.

All education and vocational training needs to emphasise care and caretaking practices, developing the capabilities of each person to hone their caring skills, while insisting that learning is about enhancing old as well as discovering new ways to nurture life and the world – whether in the sciences, humanities, carpentry or cooking. Indeed, from early on the caring state cultivates everyone's capacity to care by providing relevant education and the necessary conditions for mutual thriving. Such attempts were not only pioneered in those community nurseries set up by feminists in the 1970s, but, as we've seen, over the years have been the focus of disability rights activists and mental health users. Furthermore, once caring and practices of caretaking become the organising principle of states, mental health issues will wane. Much of the misery of our times is inextricably linked to the entrenchment of neoliberalism, the gig economy and a growing sense of precarity among the 99 per cent. The caring state would produce substantive solutions to the growing mental health crisis, rather than inadequate sticking plasters. We need radical and systemic transformation.

Given our interdependencies, each and every citizen of the caring state must be recognised as having something of significance and value to contribute at every stage of life. Thus, a transformation of cultural norms goes hand in hand with the state's avowal of everybody's intrinsic dependency, with autonomy and dependency seen as two sides of the same coin.

Significantly rethinking the welfare state in this way also moves us well beyond the traditional domestic and gendered division of labour, since both the need to care and the need for care are understood to be shared by all. This is why rethinking the welfare state is also about rethinking how public provision is conceived and distributed. The caring state is precisely not a paternal, racist or settler-colonial state. Public provision in the caring state does not revolve around deepening dependencies but rather enables everyone to cultivate what disability studies have called 'strategic autonomy and independence', while creating the conditions that allow for new relationships within and among the state and its diverse communities – relationships predicated on everyone receiving what they need both to thrive and to participate in democratic practices.

In other words, the state, while necessary to manage the smooth provision of services and resources that enable communities and caring markets to thrive, must also be responsible for facilitating more, rather than less, democratic participation. A caring state is not a verical, top-down, disciplinary or coercive one, but instead facilitates what Davina Cooper calls 'the creative, horizontal and ecological tending of present and future'.[2] A caring state necessarily works in the vein of social justice rather than criminal justice, learning the lessons of abolitionist feminism to build supportive communities rather than privatised systems of incarceration. It also imaginatively encourages 'common uses and spaces' by providing open institutions and resources which can be overseen by citizens through participatory democratic processes, such as citizens' assemblies. The caring state, in short, ensures the resourcing necessary for promiscuous care alongside caring communities to thrive.

There is copious evidence that democratically controlled, collectively resourced public services produce greater satisfaction than profit-seeking, commercialised services.[3] They significantly reduce inequality and secure broader solidarity and support, whatever the tensions they might also generate. A caring state is therefore one that provides the conditions allowing for such tensions, disagreements and ambivalences to emerge, since this encourages deliberation and concerted action. This means fostering institutions, norms, and communities that are well resourced and thus best positioned to enable us to work through at least some of the tensions of routine caring interactions. Consequently, state provision of care services is not enough without transforming its modes of delivery.

A caring infrastructure also entails shorter hours in paid work, to allow adequate time as well as resources for people to expand their capacity to care, whether in familial or any other caretaking settings. The best of hands-on care requires the time to slow down and maintain relational continuity while patiently taking stock of others in order to enable those being cared for to use or develop whatever scope they have for personal agency and well-being. This is why shorter working hours – as popularised by the campaign for the four-day week – is also key to facilitating the conditions that can educate and expand our capacities for caring, encouraging mutual participation in democratic deliberations as an integral part of the provision or need for care.[4] Once care is prioritised in this way, it becomes easier to find ways to recognise and try to meet our shifting dependencies, assisting those who need to develop or gain control over capabilities others can take for granted.

From Welfare State to Caring State

Facing collapsing infrastructures and calamities of care and livelihoods, there have already been moves to rethink policies and practices in certain cities and municipalities, although rarely on a national level. Some administrative regions have begun to offer more support for co-operative grassroots initiatives for jobs and services, both little and large, as we saw pioneered in Cleveland in the US and more recently in Preston in the UK. With homelessness a pressing problem of our time, assistance with community housing projects has also been growing, while the exemplary Social Services and Wellbeing Act passed in Wales in 2014 specifically requires local authorities to promote the development of community and user-owned services. Such modes of care can in principle not only encourage less bureaucratic and more flexible targeted services and support, but help build that vital sense of solidarity, agency, community and belonging necessary for sustaining resource building and caretaking. We can learn from and build on examples such as these. A caring state would facilitate and help resource precisely these kinds of horizontal and community-oriented projects, ensuring affordable and decent housing for all, while the relationships between the different levels and scales of governance would, of necessity, be ones of mutual responsibility but also – and crucially – subjected to continual debate and reflection.

The idea that we are all entitled to equal access to public resources when we need them will not banish all of our fears surrounding fragility and dependence. But it is the only way to lessen these fears and nurture belief in our shared humanity and interdependence, whatever our pluralities and shifting needs, especially those we have been encouraged to disavow and disparage. Insisting on such priorities would offer reassurance that those we care most about could always find forms of support, even if we cannot provide it ourselves. Above all, prioritising care would also offer the vast comfort of knowing we live in a world that is capable of valuing all living things within it and, just as importantly, that works to repair and replenish the resources we rely upon, whether ecological, manufactured or self-fashioned.

Such a world clearly rids us of old forms of state paternalism with its gendered, ethnic and racial exploitations, challenging ingrained and recently mounting ethno-nationalism by creating more porous borders for the movement of people, while deepening democratic practices on all levels of society. The caring state therefore not only builds and cultivates an infrastructure of care from cradle to grave, it also engenders new conceptions of belonging, citizenship, and rights through necessarily providing for the basic needs of all. A caring state is ultimately based on a sense of solidarity towards all its inhabitants, while also enabling what Joan Tronto calls 'caring with', the idea that citizens should care not only for other citizens but for democracy itself.

Thus, belonging, citizenship, and rights must all be organised around the principle of care rather than by birthplace, identity or national territorial claims, so that a commitment to care will be the only pledge of allegiance necessary to live in the caring state's domain. Too many of those who have provided and continue to provide the bulk of caring work in wealthier countries have been denied citizenship, even though they sometimes arrived as children. This was the case in the recent Windrush scandal in Britain, where West Indian migrants who had lived in the UK since childhood were unlawfully detained, denied legal rights and in some cases deported in the 'hostile environment' imposed by the Home Office. In contrast, new notions of caring citizens and citizenship would not only help atone for these and other past violations but completely alter our present and future notions of belonging.

This is not an impossible dream. Here, as with notions of belonging, we have much to learn from the history of Indigenous struggle against settler colonialism and extractive capitalism. In the fight against the Dakota Access Pipeline, for instance, Indigenous nations from across North America and beyond established the treaty camps at Standing Rock. Despite a devastating history of genocide and serial betrayals by the US government, the camp was not exclusive to Native Americans. Anyone was welcome so long as they adhered to the values of the camp, which included a commitment to protect the water and Mother Earth. As the historian Nick Estes states, whatever their shortcomings, the treaty camps offered a vision for an alternative future. There, 'free food, free education, free health care, free legal aid, a strong sense of community, safety, and security were guaranteed to all.'[5] In other words, they were designed according to need, not profit. The camps were built on caretaking and enshrined a radically different vision of belonging, as well as of relating to other people and the world.

Through the creation and resourcing of a caring infrastructure, rejecting all past and current state violence, states can and must be transformed. This will involve giving priority to those who have historically been most marginalised, and recognising the right of every inhabitant of the state to care and be cared for in all care's various meanings and manifestations. Adopting some of the premises of post-war welfare states, but refusing their traditional racialised policies, rigid hierarchies and sexual and racial divisions of labour, our progressive vision of states would undermine the conditions that produce economic and environmental refugees and migrants. Indeed, if care were to become the organising principle of all states across the globe, economic inequality and mass migration would decrease and environmental injustice would be rectified through our mutual commitment to caring for the world. Ultimately, then, our caring imaginaries must move away from only caring for one's own, towards the community-building of radical municipalism and nation states, ending with caring for the furthest reaches of our interconnected planet. Making this a reality necessarily involves rethinking and tackling our uncaring economies.

5

Caring Economies

What would a caring economy look like? First and foremost, it means reimagining the economy as everything that enables us to take care of each other. It would foreground and embrace the diversity of our care needs and the ways in which these needs are provisioned, not just through market exchange but also in our households, communities, states, and the world. As we have discussed previously, we must stop neoliberal capitalism from pushing the 'free market' to expand aggressively into all aspects of human economic activity.

Our vision of a caring economy also runs contrary to some Marxist economists who, in their attempt to redress the neoliberal agenda of market expansion, insist on narrowing the economic to market phenomena alone. Both these perspectives can be equally guilty of reductive assumptions. We need to reimagine the nature and scope of the economic so as to re-embed it in a society where care really is its organising principle, and 'universal care' its underlying model. Following the work of various alternative, socialist and feminist economists, including J. K. Gibson-Graham, Ann Pettifor, Nancy Folbre, Riane Eisler, Kate Raworth and those in the Women's Budget Group, we argue for a different economic vision that places all economic activity – from household to state provisioning – within a capacious understanding of society, and which is in turn understood as part of the ecology of the living world.

To act on this, we need first to restrict the power and reach of capitalist markets, and to rewrite the cultural and legal rules that dictate their (dis)embeddedness in care activity across our scales. Second, as David Harvey puts it, we need to 'go behind the veil, the fetishism of the market' to reconnect consumers with producers, and care-receivers with caregivers.[1] By so doing we can begin to enact eco-socialist alternatives to current capitalist markets, working towards caring exchange arrangements that are infinitely more democratic, solidary, and based on egalitarian modes of ownership, production and consumption across local, national and, ultimately, international levels.

Capitalist Markets: 'Free' from Whom?

Although ideologically portrayed as 'free' from the forces of the state and society, the archetypal free market has never existed. Today's capitalist free markets are quintessential systems of moneyed class domination, rather than of societal welfare maximisation through Adam Smith's famous notion of the 'invisible hand'. The prevalence of such a free-market system has been anything but a natural outcome. It has been actively enabled *by* national governments and transnational institutions such as the International Monetary Fund, from Pinochet's Chile to Greece's catastrophic austerity programmes in response to the 2008–09 financial crisis.

The case of crisis-hit Greece is extreme, yet particularly illustrative. Having been forced by the so-called troika (International Monetary Fund, European Commission and European Central Bank) to undergo a neoliberal economic makeover, the country ended up losing more than 30 per cent of its GDP, while its national debt nearly doubled to 190 per cent in just over five years. And yet, the stubbornly neoliberal demands of the troika included marketising or semi-marketising just about everything, from Greece's health and educational infrastructures to public water and community infrastructures. Consequently, the country experienced unprecedented deterioration of its care infrastructures and overall quality of care provision (a deterioration that Greece was painfully aware of in its response to the coronavirus crisis). For instance, between 2010 and 2012, alongside the damning economic indicators, suicide and depression rates increased by over 35 per cent in just over two years; HIV infections from drug use increased by over 400 per cent. In effect the country witnessed, violently and abruptly, a systemic reconfiguration of what the United Nations economist Shahra Razavi would describe as its 'care diamond': a society's shifting provision of care across the four key sectors of households, communities, state and markets. Nowadays, in Greece and beyond, what is left outside markets is devalued and delegated to the other sectors of the diamond: mostly to families, but also to communities. The neoliberal market does not – indeed cannot – value personal engagement, emotional connection, commitment, empathy or attentiveness, unless contracted for financial rewards.

But the case of Greece also vividly illustrated what economic historians and anthropologists have long emphasised, which is that neoliberalism's project to expand the archetypal model of 'free markets' can never be complete. All market systems have, always and everywhere, been embedded in societal laws, regulations, policies and cultures. To varying degrees, 'free' neoliberal markets will always be subjected to scrutiny by the people they are supposed to serve.

Accordingly, what we witnessed on the ground in Greece was a radical proliferation of solidarity and alternative economic networks that were both products of the economic crisis and endeavours to fill the gaps left by the failures of neoliberalism. Marketised relations gave way to voluntary networks of care, mutuality and interdependency. It is estimated that between 2011 and 2014, Greece witnessed the emergence of forty-seven self-managed food banks; twenty-one solidarity kitchens distributing hundreds of food parcels every week; forty-five without-middlemen distribution networks with more than 5,000 tons of distributed products; and around thirty solidarity education initiatives.

Importantly, these alternative systems of exchange were experienced as infinitely more caring, reliant as they were on horizontal models of collaboration rather than top-down control. Decisions were usually taken by consensus, in weekly or bi-weekly assemblies; there were no organisational hierarchies, and any profits or commercialised activities were strictly prohibited. These kinds of initiatives were not just about creating more socially and environmentally equitable alternatives. They were also about caring and protecting participants from the bitter aura of neoliberal violence, characterised by overwhelming feelings of powerlessness, social isolation, and fear. They helped to cultivate caring, collective communities. As one leaflet produced by the Athens-based anti-consumerist collective Skoros put it: 'We are definitely not mourning the loss of our spending power . . . We believe in solidarity, social support and collaboration.'

Care Logics Versus Market Logics

Some economists argue that the model of commoditised care can be successful, even desirable, under some circumstances – for instance when it comes to impersonal, standardised tasks (such as cleaning) or technology-mediated care (such as health screening devices or home automation for the elderly and disabled). But such a model is woefully inadequate. Care and capitalist market logics cannot be reconciled.

First, there are few forms of intimate care work that are not best delivered with personal engagement and emotional attachment. Hands-on care – or 'care for', in Joan Tronto's terms – therefore differs from any other 'thing' or commodity, since it is more often than not 'sticky' for both the carers and those cared for, as they enter relationships that can only flourish under the auspices of mutuality, endurance and patience. Market logics do not have the vocabulary, let alone the capacity, to capture or measure such values. As the feminist economist Nancy Folbre puts it, we should be thinking of 'invisible hearts', not 'invisible hands', when it comes to how care often is, and indeed should be, organised. That is, we should fully acknowledge that the forces of care and compassion must always override the market-mediated forces of individualised self-interest. Our model of universal care is a key step towards resolving this economic paradox.

Second, markets can only allocate care responsibilities and services on the basis of purchasing power. Those with higher capital are always the winners. 'Losers' are all those with limited, if any, access to markets, especially if they also have limited access to care within their kinship structures or communities. The market-mediated distribution of care services not only reflects but also hugely exacerbates previous income inequalities and care deficits. Those with high incomes will be able to fulfil a range of care needs, from high-quality education to housing, enabling a virtuous circle of investment in what has come to be understood as 'human capital'. Even having time to care for oneself is often viewed as a form of luxury nowadays, one restricted to those that can comfortably invest in contemporary retreats or the wellness centres of the booming self-care industry. Equal access to material, social, and environmental resources is fundamental to a caring economy.

Third, market norms are notorious for 'crowding out' non-market values. Valuing care is clearly not the same as marketising care. Marketising care foregrounds self-interest and instrumentality in every sphere of our (un)caring lives. Inevitably, both the even distribution of care work and its quality decline. Think, for instance, of a nanny who does anything the kids want with a view to increase their ratings on care.com; a medical doctor working in private practice who is keen to process as many patients as possible with a view to increase their daily targets; or a university lecturer who is inflating student marks in order to get better evaluations and thus apply for a promotion. Only by confronting, resisting and eliminating market metrics and corporate power can caring values be allowed to flourish. This is another reason to insist upon the universal care model: so that care work may be valued highly and care resources distributed equally, without being subjected to capitalist market principles of supply and demand.

Demarketising Care Infrastructures

What is to be done about the endemic carelessness of capitalist markets? And how do we stop their ruthless expansion into every sphere of our caring lives? We need a two-pronged strategy: first, we urgently need to push back against the reckless and destructive marketisation of all our care sectors and infrastructures; second, we have to start building more caring, equitable and eco-socialist alternatives to capitalist markets.

Re-socialising and insourcing (rather than outsourcing) our care commons and infrastructures is a key precondition for the road towards more caring economies. Key sectors of our economy, such as health, education and housing, have been subjected, for far too long, to the neoliberal dogma of relentless marketisation and privatisation. Arguably nothing illustrated this more strongly than the coronavirus crisis. In the course of a few weeks, most economically advanced nations began reinvesting massively in their national health systems and walking away from public–private partnerships that had so dangerously prioritised the interests of businesses over the public good. Countries like Spain nationalised all their private hospitals and healthcare providers; many other countries, including the US and the UK, redirected industrial production towards supplying masks and ventilators. Put differently, the irreconcilability of care with market logics hit home.

At the same time, however – and precisely due to the ingrained nature of marketised logics – it did not hit home hard enough. Fierce internal markets for hospital protective equipment (PPE) and ventilators raised their cost in the US; and in the UK, the failure of the government to order corporations to comply, and to use the resources of the EU and the public sector, resulted in a catastrophic lack of care for frontline healthcare workers.[2]

We need to demarketise our care infrastructures, in all their diversity and complexity. But once we acknowledge that markets of some sort, where goods and services are exchanged, will always have a key role to play in the redistribution of resources, we also need to rethink and reconfigure their broader place in a caring society. As Kate Raworth puts it, we need to *re-regulate* them, acknowledging that all markets – capitalist or otherwise – are already embedded in a specific set of legal, political and cultural regulations. In reconfiguring the role of markets, we need to ensure that it is people and the planet that benefit from their distributive function, not the moneyed class.

Re-regulating Markets and Defetishising Commodities

The re-regulation and thus the reconfiguration of markets can take many different forms: co-operatives, nationalisation, progressive municipalism, localisation, insourcing, public–commons partnerships. All are ways in which our markets, our means of production and consumption, can be collectivised and socialised as well as democratised. Through all these strategies and more, we need to ensure that consumers are reconnected with producers, and care-receivers with caregivers. In other words, we need to defetishise markets, which is to say reverse the replacement of social relations with relations among commodities, and of care values with exchange value. This has long been the agenda of various bottom-up initiatives, from the small structure in Athens that directly link Zapatista producers with Greek consumers, to the already scaled-up solidarity economy structures of Spain, now accounting for roughly 10 per cent of the country's GDP.

The need to defetishise and increase accountability along the lengthy commodity chains of human and non-human exploitation has also been the aim of some of the more progressive examples of Fairtrade practice, which have supported workers' co-operatives around the globe. But Fairtrade can exist as a niche product within an otherwise regressive and exploitative capitalist economy.

Defetishisation therefore needs to be produced through more stringent, all-encompassing *re-regulation*. Current laws and regulations need radically expanding, improving and shifting beyond neoliberal use. The UK's Modern Slavery Act and the California Transparency in Supply Chains Act, for instance, make a start but fall well short of radically countering neoliberal market logics, given that they rely on the goodwill of NGOs and 'consumers' for their enforcement. In so doing they build upon a longer history of both corporate and governmental efforts to generate greater consumer responsibility, as part of attempts to deflect from their own responsibilities. Ordinary people should not be made to feel responsible or guilty for such systemic carelessness. We need to prioritise a model of caring citizenship rather than individualist consumer choices. It is only through demanding increased and expansive defetishisation – rather than the selective transparency advocated by some business and governmental actors – that we can begin to address the abject failures of care that are endemic in our current system.

Caring, eco-socialist markets would also have to address modes of ownership, production and consumption.

Common to all existing alternatives (from nationalising public resources to worker co-ops) is the need for re-regulated and democratically governed markets that are as egalitarian, participatory and environmentally sustainable as possible. Our social and planetary concerns must come before profits. We need caring economic arrangements that focus on co-operative networks of mutual support and which attempt to redistribute social and material wealth according to everyone's care needs. Today, this wealth has instead been appropriated globally and divided among the capitalist class on a historically unprecedented scale.

One structure that moves in the right direction is the co-operative; including, as we've seen, Mondragon, the world's largest and most successful federation of worker-owned co-operatives, which emerged in the 1950s in response to the fascist regime of General Franco and today employs over 74,000 workers. Indeed, it now articulates a network of over 100 constituent worker co-operatives, working in a range of sectors, from agriculture and retail to a bank and a university, and it is one of the ten largest companies in Spain. Globally, there are many more examples of such co-operation, care, worker respect, democracy and environmental sustainability emerging from below. The seeds of bottom-up socioeconomic change have long histories and are sprouting in many places. This is captured by the famous slogan – attributed to a 1978 poem by Dinos Christianopoulos – often quoted by solidarity economy activists around the globe: 'What didn't you do to bury me / But you forgot that I was a seed!'

Finally, wherever possible, markets should also be locally embedded. Local markets are better suited for cultivating relationships among producers, traders and consumers. They can address local needs, stimulate placemaking and community-making and provide a shield against the interests of transnational capital, making them better suited for (caring) purposes. They are more likely to be deeply entrenched within an ideology of sustainability and translocal solidarity, rather than being driven by parochial or paternalistic logics. As Colin Hines, a co-founder of the Green New Deal group, has long argued, the regeneration of local economies has the potential to rehumanise trade, and counter the systemic abuse of worker and environmental rights in both the Global North and South. To do so, market localisation has to be part of a progressive, transnational culture of solidarity. And as we began to discuss earlier, the climate crisis means that, especially in the Global North, we need to drastically cut our carbon-heavy consumer habits.

And yet, just as the boundaries of current markets are constantly evolving, with national governments unwilling to confront transnational capital, our attempts to reimagine and redraw those boundaries must also evolve. We can start by working to eliminate the shadow economies and deregulated financial markets now dominating care provision, which are little understood, let alone made accountable. As Ann Pettifor has recently illustrated in *The Case for the New Green Deal*, shadow banking – the activities of offshore financial entities operating outside the regulation of any state – now amounts to $185 trillion, roughly three times the world's GDP. Yet these bank-like entities rely upon and survive through the safety of public financial assets, supported by ordinary taxpayers. Offshore capital must be brought back onshore and used for our collective benefit, not that of the global elite.[3]

The rise of algorithmic capitalism and the appropriation of digital commons pose further challenges for our progressive model of care, with their surveillance of our caring activities via increasingly sophisticated data analytics that escape our sphere of comprehension. Big data and artificial intelligence are already actively shaping our (caring) lives – from manipulating public opinion to data devices that may be (un)caring 'by design' (for example, smart fridges that avoid environmental and supply chain transparency).[4]

As with offline commons, we need to insist that our online or digital commons are democratised, publicly and collectively owned and managed modes of production, involving peer-to-peer production (P2P). These should include, for instance, nationalising broadband and other digital infrastructures. Likewise, 'platform co-operativism' – as a counterproposal to capitalist innovations such as Facebook, YouTube, Uber and Airbnb – is fundamental to creating a caring economy. For example, Fairbnb, an ethical home-sharing site, directly challenges Airbnb's business model with the aim of returning half the commissions charged to the local community for sustainable projects. The platform is co-owned and co-governed by those who work in it, use it or are impacted by its use. More progressively still, and drawing upon the principles of radical municipalism, Barcelona has actively encouraged an alliance between platform co-operativists, labour organisations and communities. This includes supporting co-operative solutions that are collectivised and democratically controlled through citizen-governed digital infrastructures.[5]

In all these ways our markets and economies can become more caring. Constructing and nurturing the commons, and collectivising spheres of production and consumption, are key to creating an eco-socialist economy that is able to care. This includes encouraging the defetishisation, re-regulation, and localisation of markets, and more democratic, socialised and egalitarian modes of ownership, from co-operatives and insourcing to nationalisation of key services. At the same time, we need to *demarketise* key areas of our economy and to counter the out-of-control privatisation and financialisation of our care infrastructures. But more caring, eco-socialist markets can only be created by carefully controlled and democratised economies: systems that do not function at the expense of people or the planet.

6

Caring for the World

Our Extensive Interdependence

How can we create a more caring world, one capable of sustaining and nourishing all forms of life?

Addressing the problems of carelessness on a global scale returns us to a 'politics of interdependence', to the inescapable fact that we live in an interconnected and complex world. This has been demonstrated abruptly and devastatingly by the Covid-19 pandemic that moved so rapidly across borders. After all, different decisions made at state level and shaped by distinct national priorities – whether the protection of capitalist wealth or concern with healthcare workers – have affected both the global life of the virus and our own life chances. Simultaneously, the global lockdown has paradoxically given us sudden, fragmented glimpses of how we *could* create better worlds. We have witnessed the sharing of equipment between nations, improved air quality, local mutual aid practices, and reduced working hours. We have also witnessed grateful recognition of the value of hands-on care and other forms of essential work.

The pandemic, in short, has dramatically and tragically highlighted many of the essential functions that are crucial for our web of life to be sustained: the labour of nurses and doctors, delivery drivers and garbage collectors. But it has also exposed how vital transnational alliances and co-operation are.

To bring our world back from the brink of catastrophe, care needs to be prioritised and worked through on all scales, levels and dimensions: from kinships to communities, from states to transnational strategies – currently the arena of global corporations and financial capital. It is the realities of global inequality that underlie so much devastation in our world today. Thus, in order to 'scale up' our model of universal care to the global level, we need to foster transnational institutions, global networks and alliances based on the principles of interdependency and sharing resources, while embracing a democratic cosmopolitanism.

Transnational Institutions and the Global Valuation of Care

Caring capacities are shaped by nation states, but also transgress and extend beyond them. This means building new transnational institutions and intergovernmental organisations, agencies and policies whose organizing principles are based on care and caretaking and which can be reshaped according to care logics, not neoliberal capitalist logics.

So, caring for the world means nation states together rolling out a Green New Deal. Over recent decades, this has evolved as a multifaceted social justice strategy to deal with climate crisis through joined-up policies restructuring work, energy and financial systems. The evolution of the idea is itself intra- and transnational. It appeared in different manifestations in the UK in the 2000s, when a particular, internationalist version was codified by a group including environmental NGO workers, trade unionists and economists. In the 2010s, a more domestic variant was reignited in the US by Alexandria Ocasio-Cortez and her team.[1]

Today the Green New Deal is a crucial part of the imaginary of the international left because it is rightly understood as a humane, feasible, affordable and achievable way to address the nightmare of planetary climate crisis. Fundamental to its programme is the decarbonising of energy systems: leaving fossil fuels in the ground and investing in renewables on a massive scale. The Green New Deal involves changes in patterns of work, both with the creation of more 'green jobs' – through the vast expansion of renewables, conservation, tree planting and re-wilding – and the reduction of the working week to lower emissions and expand our time and ability to care.

But the Green New Deal alone is not enough. We urgently need the creation of global left alliances that will directly counter the current authoritarian front. The Progressive International, an initiative led by Bernie Sanders and Yannis Varoufakis that aims to unite progressive left-wing activists and organisations, is just one potentially good example. We also need an array of transnational institutions and agencies whose organising principles are based on care and caretaking. Whatever its current limitations, we see this in the World Health Organisation, whose transnational remit Donald Trump has been desperately trying to undermine. We also see certain aspects of global progressive alliances in the sustainable development projects focusing on the needs of poorer countries supported by the educational wing of the UN, including the World Institute for Development Economics Research (WIDER), in which the Indian economist and philosopher Amartya Sen has played such a prominent role. It was in WIDER that Sen first developed his influential 'Capability Approach' in the 1980s, redefining 'poverty' in terms of the deprivation of the capacity to live a good life, while broadening the notion of 'development' beyond the economic to include expanding the capabilities of people, wherever they live, to participate in social life. This capabilities approach is now being embraced by progressive networks worldwide.

We need to build on these existing progressive transnational institutions so that they reflect the needs of all populations around the globe, rather than do the bidding of the most powerful. Indeed, it is global corporations and financial institutions, loosely tied to powerful nation states, that have been responsible for so much environmental wreckage up until now. Environmental devastation, as we know, disproportionately affects the world's poorest economies and populations. These struggling economies are frequently the legacy of Western imperialism and neo-colonialism, former colonial territories that have for decades been sapped by debt repayments, undermining their service infrastructures and leaving so many destitute. Prioritising global care necessarily means tackling global inequality.

Oxfam's recent report *Time to Care* highlights the need to deal with the care crisis by addressing global inequalities of wealth and value through progressive taxation. We need immediate debt cancellation as well as politicians and policies that will tax the billionaires and recognise that 'every billionaire is a policy failure'. It means combating the likes of Amazon CEO Jeff Bezos, who has amassed an extra $24 billion during the pandemic, even as he refuses to pay sick leave to his employees. Dealing with global inequality therefore involves radically restructuring our national but also international financial institutions, so that they do not channel money to the offshore global elite but instead invest in the care of people, communities and the planet.

Currently, financial deregulation stimulates expansive credit and environmentally unsustainable consumption; financial fraud has effectively become decriminalised; and the hegemony of the US dollar boosts both. A third of the world's wealth is currently held offshore. Just as we need to *insource* rather than *outsource* at local and community levels, so too do we need to 'reshore' finance in order to bring these unaccountable billionaires back to regulation by nation states. This also means, as we've already shown, engaging with the ideas of feminist economists and degrowth and environmental activists who model ways of both regenerating the biodiversity of our planet and redistributing global wealth. Nation states can and must put 'sand in the wheels' of the global elite, through, for instance, an international financial transactions tax that redistributes their revenues, as proposed by the US economist James Tobin, and currently supported by many European states. Caring for the world involves remaking and democratising all international institutions and networks, so that they facilitate the redistribution of the world's resources, enabling all states and their populations to build the caring and sharing infrastructure that they need to thrive.

A Global Alliance of Caring Connections

Progressive transnational networks can also build upon those that currently exist. After all, progressive change will not just happen without huge numbers of us pushing for it in all kinds of contexts, even though tackling the carelessness with which we have treated the planet cannot simply be undertaken at the neighbourhood or individual level, but requires state and international intervention.

Caring for the world, then, means rebuilding and democratising social infrastructures and shared spaces across all scales, expanding support of and alliances with progressive movements and institutions in the process. The demand for such transformation often begins from combative grassroots resistance, as we saw in the recent explosion of activism against climate change and the loss of biodiversity, most dramatically in the confrontations and occupations organised by Extinction Rebellion (XR) during 2019. These actions contributed towards parliamentary decisions in several countries (including Bangladesh, the UK, Portugal, France and Argentina) which declared a climate emergency a few months later.

Historically, grassroots resistance has often produced quite surprising results, at least temporarily, whether toppling oppressive regimes, as in the Arab Spring of 2012, or holding back the environmental hazards stemming from pipeline installation, mining, fracking, deforestation or dam building. As Rebecca Solnit suggests, 'every protest shifts the world's balance', or has the potential to do so. Modes of resistance in one place, even when repressed, can leap borders, sprouting up in other forms in a different locale or even in another part of the world. For instance, recent popular uprisings in South America, especially Chile, were inspired by those in the Arab world. Resistance to the Dakota Access Pipeline to transport oil and cut across native land at Standing Rock inspired Alexandria Ocasio-Cortez to run for office. While activism on the ground, like Standing Rock, has brought new hope and power to Native Americans in protecting their land, it has also helped to inspire those working to create legislation around Green New Deals at government levels.

Thus, we need to build on all the progressive transnational networks that currently exist, from radical municipal movements like Fearless Cities to global workers' coalitions, such as the International Trade Union Confederation (ITUC) and other global union federations (GUFs). There are also numerous transnational feminist justice and peace networks, most prominent recently being the Women's March and Women's Strike movements. The Global Women's Strike was prompted in part by the October 2016 Polish women's nationwide strike on 'Black Monday', against the right-wing Polish government's consideration of criminalising abortion, and the #NiUnaMenos ('Not one woman less') protests against femicide, the killing of women, in Argentina, Mexico, Chile, El Salvador and Brazil. The UK and US branches clearly link their actions to other mass mobilisations across the globe organised by women, while focusing particularly on the world's dependence on women's unpaid or low-paid caring activities. We can also learn, and celebrate, whenever we see the integration of progressive ethics into state policy. Countries such as New Zealand and Finland have taken the lead by integrating educational materials on climate change and environmental protection into the school curriculum.

Recalling past and acknowledging recent transnational fertilisations at the level of social movements are then crucial, because they highlight the need to build upon the ties that already bind us. But to understand the planetary dimension of care and shared global ecologies we also need to transform the way in which we understand borders, as well as cultivate a radically democratic everyday cosmopolitanism. This is particularly urgent during a period which has seen a rise in racist and xenophobic right-wing populism.

Borders

At the heart of *The Care Manifesto* is the demand to distribute the world's resources not only in an environmentally sustainable fashion but also in ways that more equitably sustain populations and diminish the resentment between them to create connections across difference.

Not only do nation states need to care about their own citizens, they also need to attend to others: asylum seekers and migrants. More porous borders between nation states are therefore vital to achieve a more caring world. In its own skewed way, neoliberalism seeks to eliminate borders, albeit in a fashion favouring capital over labour, which in turn has caused the highly uneven, hostile and racialised border regimes we see today. However, if we want democratically accountable, caring states to replace financial markets as the privileged site of resource distribution, then we need fundamentally different kinds of borders.

Borders should return to the edges of nation states, and be radically reduced, rather than create internal divisions that feed into our ultra-nationalist moment. This means an end to using citizens as border guards, as well as the elimination of 'grey zones' in which refugees and other migrants exist in a liminal state of seemingly perpetual statelessness. Borders should be permeable to all who wish to cross them, and co-ordinated transnationally to ensure migration does not drain certain parts of the world of a needed population while overcrowding others. This will only be possible if the conditions that force people to flee their homes due to penury, war or climate events are significantly diminished – returning us full circle to the Green New Deal, in order to address inequality and create an equitability of care. Indeed, this brings us full circle to our ineluctable interdependencies, if we hope to encourage fulfilling lives in a sustainable world.

The Interdependence of Care

Building a caring world thus returns us to where our manifesto began: from acting upon the understanding that as living creatures we exist alongside and in connection with all other human and non-human beings, and also remain dependent upon the systems and networks, animate and inanimate, that sustain life across the planet. We recognise that we are all inevitably steeped in ambivalence and even aggression towards others. This is particularly likely to be true in relation to those who are most distant and unknown to us, but it may also apply in relation to those who are closest, even if such ambivalences are often suppressed. Yet, as Judith Butler argues, this is precisely why it is only once we recognise our shared entanglement in conflict – along with its powerful corollary, an awareness of our shared vulnerability and interdependence – that we can begin to develop new caring imaginaries on a global scale.[2]

Creating such a caring world means first and foremost avowing our interdependences and cultivating a far-reaching ethics of care and solidarity in all our relationships: from our social movements, through relationships between nation states, to non-human life and the planet. Caring societies can only be built by overcoming care*less* nationalist imaginaries and fostering truly transnational outlooks among radically democratic cosmopolitan subjects, people who care across difference and distance.

A truly global politics, then, requires embracing what we call an everyday cosmopolitanism – promiscuous care on a global scale – that moves our caring imaginaries beyond kinship structures, communities and nation states to the furthest reaches of the 'strangest' parts of the planet. Cosmopolitan subjects who are, literally, 'citizens of the world', have care for the world in their hearts.

While care for strangers may seem a hard emotion to cultivate, developing a comfort with the foreign or alien is not actually beyond us. Forms of everyday cosmopolitanism emerge quite spontaneously in the lives of cities, where people historically considered strangers to one another intermingle and combine in the course of their daily lives. Paul Gilroy calls this 'convivial culture', Mica Nava 'visceral cosmopolitanism'.[3]

The *caring* cosmopolitan subject is precisely not the wealthy person moving across the globe with little care for the people or places they encounter, but one who sees through the hollow certainties of nationalism and cultivates a transnational orientation of care towards the stranger. Being cosmopolitan means being at ease with strangeness; knowing that we have no choice but to live with difference, whatever differences come to matter in specific times and places.

Afterthoughts

The Care Manifesto offers a queer–feminist–anti-racist–eco-socialist political vision of 'universal care'. Universal care means we are all jointly responsible for hands-on care work, as well as engaging with and caring about the flourishing of other people and the planet. It means reclaiming forms of genuinely collective and communal life, adopting alternatives to capitalist markets, and reversing the marketisation of care infrastructures. It also means restoring and radically deepening our welfare states, both centrally and locally. And, finally, it means creating Green New Deals at the transnational level, caring international institutions and more porous borders, and cultivating everyday cosmopolitanism.

We conclude our manifesto at a time of unprecedented worldwide lockdowns. As we've shown, the Covid-19 pandemic has certainly laid bare the horrors of neoliberalism. But it has also revitalised a conversation about care, however limited it may still be.

The current global calamity is clearly a moment of profound rupture. Historically, ruptures have paved the way for radical progressive change, as happened in the wake of World War II with the growth of welfare in many Western states, and successful independence struggles in former European colonies. But ruptures have also triggered the growth of nationalism, authoritarianism and a rebooted capitalism, as in the wake of the 2007–08 financial crisis.

The challenge today is to build upon earlier moments of radical change. Achieving the vision we've laid out in this manifesto necessarily means organising to ensure that the legacy of Covid-19 is not an intensified neoliberal authoritarianism but a new politics, where care is central at every level. We know this vision of universal care is as daunting as it is pressing. But in our current moment of rupture, where neoliberal norms are crumbling, we have a rare opportunity. Awareness of our systemic carelessness across all social hierarchies has begun to appear everywhere. Let's begin by avowing care, in all of its ubiquitous complexities, and by building more enduring and participatory caring outlooks, contexts and infrastructures, wherever we can.

Acknowledgements

We are very grateful to Rosie Warren and Leo Hollis at Verso for encouraging us to write *The Care Manifesto,* and supporting us throughout. We also want to thank Sue Himmelweit, Neve Gordon, Alan Bradshaw and Jeremy Gilbert for reading and commenting on this work at different stages. We are very grateful to the people who invited us to talk, to share ideas, and who hosted us in various locations: Helen Wood and CAMEO in Leicester; Agnes Bolsø and Siri Øyslebø Sørensen in Norway; Beverley Skeggs (and her wider care group); Sarah Banet-Weiser at the LSE; and Jonathan Gross, both at Birkbeck and at the HDCA conference. Thanks as well to Lorna Scott-Fox for excellent copy-editing. We are indebted to the ideas of many others working in differing ways on care, who cannot be named within the tight framings of a manifesto. Finally, our thanks to our colleagues, extended families and friends – and especially Davide, Joe and Noah – for their on-going support and, most of all, for all their care.

References

Preface

1. Helen Wood and Beverley Skeggs, 'Clap for carers? From care gratitude to care justice', *European Journal of Cultural Studies* 23 (4) (2020): 641–7.
2. See, for example, Rianne Mahon and Juliana Martinez Franzoni, 'Special Section on *The Care Manifesto: The Politics of Interdependence*', *Social Politics: International Studies in Gender, State & Society* 28 (4) (2021): 831–3; and the European YOU(th) CARE for Change Project.
3. See Joel Bakan, Andreas Chatzidakis and Jo Littler (eds), *The Moralizing Corporation: The Rise and Fall of Corporate Carewashing*, Bristol University Press (2016).
4. Emily Kos, Nan DasGupta, Gabrielle Novacek, and Rohan Sajdeh, 'To Fix the Labor Shortage, Solve the Care Crisis', Boston Consulting Group, 19 May 2022.
5. Arunima Kumar and Anousha Sakoui, 'BP to ditch renewable goales and retun focus to fossil fuel', Reuters, 24 February 2025.
6. Human Rights Council, 'From economy of occupation to economy of genocide', UN.org, 16 June–11 July 2025.
7. Simon Jessop and Victoria Furness, 'HSBC joins US banks in quitting climate coalition', Reuters, 11 July 2025.

8. Judith Butler, 'Trump is unleashing sadism upon the world. But we cannot get overwhelmed', *The Guardian*, 6 Feburary 2025.

Introduction

1. Nira Yuval-Davis, Georgie Wemyss and Kathryn Cassidy, *Bordering*, Polity Press (2019).
2. Giorgio Agamben, *Homo Sacer: Sovereign Power and Bare Life*, Stanford University Press (1998).
3. Club of Rome, *The Limits of Growth, Universe Books* (1972); Ann Pettifor, *The Case for the Green New Deal*, Verso (2019); Kate Raworth, *Doughnut Economics*, Chelsea Green Publications (2018); Naomi Klein, *On Fire*, Penguin (2019).
4. Danny Dorling, *Peak Inequality*, Policy Press (2018).
5. Women's Budget Group, *Crises Collide: Women and Covid-19* (2020).
6. Alan White, *Shadow State: Inside the Secret Companies That Run Britain*, OneWorld (2016).
7. Bev Skeggs, 'What everyone with parents is likely to face in the future', *Sociological Review*, 29 March 2019, thesociologicalreview.com. See also: Bob Hudson, *The Failure of Privatised Adult Social Care in England: What Is to Be Done?*, Centre for Health and the Public Interest (November 2016).
8. Saskia Sassen, *Losing Control? Sovereignty in the Age of Globalization*, Columbia University Press (2015); David Harvey, *Rebel Cities*, Verso (2013).

1. Caring Politics

1. Joan Tronto, *Caring Democracy: Markets, Equality, Justice*, New York University Press (2013).
2. Sarah Benton, 'Dependence', *Soundings: A Journal of Politics and Culture* 70 (Winter, 2018): 61, 62.
3. Nancy Fraser, *Fortunes of Feminism*, Verso (2013).
4. Rozsika Parker, *Torn in Two: The Experience of Maternal Ambivalence*, Virago (1995).
5. See Adolf Ratzka, 'Independent living and our organizations: a definition', independentliving.org, 1997.

2. Caring Kinships

1. Patricia Hill Collins, *Black Feminist Thought: Knowledge, Consciousness, and the Politics of Empowerment*, Routledge (2000), pp. 178–83.
2. Kath Weston, *Families We Choose: Lesbians, Gays, Kinship*, Columbia University Press (1991).
3. Sasha Roseneil and Shelley Budgeon, 'Cultures of Intimacy and Care Beyond the Family: Personal Life and Social Change in the Early 21st Century', *Current Sociology* 52(2) (2004): 153.
4. Paul Byron, *Friendship and Digital Cultures of Care*, Routledge (forthcoming).
5. Nick Estes, *Our History Is the Future*, Verso (2019), p. 256.
6. Douglas Crimp, 'How to Have Promiscuity in an Epidemic', *October* 43 (1987): 253.

3. Caring Communities

1. Massimo de Angelis, *Omnia Sunt Communia*, Zed Books (2017).
2. See Pirate Care, syllabus.pirate.care/.
3. 'Municipalism and Feminism Then and Now: Hilary Wainwright Talks to Jo Littler', *Soundings* 74 (2020): 10–25.
4. 'The GLC Story', glcstory.co.uk.
5. Kathy Williams, 'A Missing Municipalist Legacy: The GLC and the Changing Cultural Politics of the Southbank Centre', *Soundings* 74 (2020): 26–39.
6. Kirsten Forkert, *Austerity as Public Mood*, Rowman and Littlefield (2017), pp. 107–25.
7. See: Timothy Garton Ash, 'What kind of post-corona world do we Europeans want?', *openDemocracy*, 11 May 2020.
8. Nick Srnicek, *Platform Capitalism*, Polity (2016).
9. Aditya Chakrabortty, 'In 2011 Preston hit rock bottom. Then it took back control', *Guardian*, 31 January 2018, theguardian.com/commentisfree.
10. Via the Evergreen Fund for Employee Ownership. See: democracycollaborative.org.
11. Óscar García Agustín, 'New Municipalism as Space for solidarity', *Soundings* 74 (2020): 54–67.
12. Keir Milburn and Bertie Russell, 'What Can an Institution Do? Towards Public-Common Partnerships and a New Common-sense', *Renewal* 26(4) (2018): 45–55.
13. Emma Dowling, 'Confronting Capital's Care Fix: Care Through the Lens of Democracy', *Equality, Diversity*

and Inclusion: An International Journal 37(4) (2018): 332–46.

14. Matthew Lawrence, Andrew Pendleton and Sara Mahmoud, *Co-operatives Unleashed: Doubling the Size of the UK's Co-operative Sector*, New Economics Foundation (2018), p. 20.

4. Caring States

1. Sally Alexander, 'Primary maternal preoccupation: D. W. Winnicott and social democracy in mid-twentieth century Britain', in Sally Alexander and Barbara Taylor (eds), *History and Psyche: Culture, Psychoanalysis and the Past*, Palgrave Macmillan (2012).
2. Davina Cooper, *Feeling Like a State: Desire, Denial, and the Recasting of Authority*, Duke University Press (2019), p. 4.
3. Anna Coote and Andrew Percy, *The Case for Universal Basic Services*, Polity (2020).
4. Autonomy and NEF, *The Shorter Working Week: A Radical and Pragmatic Proposal* (2019).
5. Estes, *Our History Is the Future*, p. 256.

5. Caring Economies

1. David Harvey, 'Between Space and Time: Reflections on the Geographical Imagination', *Annals of the Association of American Geographers* 80(3) (1990): 418–34.
2. See: Richard Horton, 'Offline: Covid-19 and the NHS – "A national scandal"', thelancet.com, 28 March 2020.

3. See, for example: letschangetherules.org/policies-and-solutions/finance.
4. See Carole Cadwalladr, 'Fresh Cambridge Analytica leak "shows global manipulation is out of control"', *Guardian*, 4 January 2020.
5. Such as decidim.barcelona.

6. Caring for the World

1. Pettifor, *The Case for the Green New Deal.*
2. Judith Butler, *The Force of Nonviolence: The Ethical in the Political*, Verso (2020).
3. Paul Gilroy, *After Empire*, Routledge (2004); Mica Nava, *Visceral Cosmopolitanism*, Berg (2007).

Further Reading

Alexander, Sally. 'Primary Maternal Preoccupation: D. W. Winnicott and Social Democracy in Mid-Twentieth Century Britain', in Sally Alexander and Barbara Taylor (eds.). *History and Psyche: Culture, Psychoanalysis and the Past*, Palgrave Macmillan (2012): 149–72.

Anderson, Bridget. *Doing the Dirty Work? The Global Politics of Domestic Labour*. Zed (2000).

Aronoff, Kate, et al. *A Planet to Win: Why We Need a Green New Deal*. Verso (2019).

Arruzza, Cinzia, Tithi Bhattacharya and Nancy Fraser. *Feminism for the 99%: A Manifesto*. Verso (2019).

Autonomy and NEF. *The Shorter Working Week: A Radical and Pragmatic Proposal*. (2019).

Benton, Sarah. 'Dependence', *Soundings: A Journal of Politics and Culture* 70 (Winter, 2018): 61, 62.

Briggs, Laura. *How All Politics Became Reproductive Politics: From Welfare Reform to Foreclosure to Trump*. University of California Press (2018).

Butler, Judith. *The Force of Nonviolence: The Ethical in the Political*. Verso (2020).

———. *Precarious Life: The Powers of Mourning and Violence*. Verso (2004).

Byron, Paul. *Friendship and Digital Cultures of Care*. Routledge (forthcoming).

CareNotes Collective. *Care Notes: A Notebook of Health Autonomy*. Common Notions (2020).

Chatzidakis, Andreas and Deidre Shaw. 'Sustainability: Issues of Scale, Care and Consumption', *British Journal of Management* 29 (2) (2018): 299–315.

Chatzidakis, Andreas Deidre Shaw and Matthew Allen, 'A Psycho-Social Approach to Consumer Ethics', *Journal of Consumer Culture*, (2018) doi.org.

Coffey, Clare, et al. *Time to Care: Unpaid and Underpaid Care Work and the Global Inequality Crisis*. Oxfam (2020).

Cooper, Davina. *Feeling Like a State: Desire, Denial, and the Recasting of Authority*. Duke University Press (2019).

Coote, Anna and Andrew Percy. *The Case for Universal Basic Services*. Polity (2020).

Crimp, Douglas. 'How to Have Promiscuity in an Epidemic', *October* (43) (1987): 237–71.

Davis, Angela J. (ed.). *Policing the Black Man: Arrest, Prosecution, and Imprisonment*. Pantheon Books (2017).

de Angelis, Massimo. *Omnia Sunt Communia: On the Commons and the Transformation to Postcapitalism*. Zed Books (2017).

Dorling, Danny. *Peak Inequality*. Policy Press (2018).

Dowling, Emma. *The Care Crisis*. Verso (2021).

Duffy, Mignon. 'Doing the Dirty Work: Gender, Race, and Reproductive Labor in Historical Perspective', *Gender and Society* 21 (3) (2007): 313–36.

Duffy Mignon, et al. (eds.) *Caring on the Clock: The Complexities and Contradictions of Paid Care Work*. Rutgers University Press (2015).

Ehrenreich, Barbara. *Nickel and Dimed: On (Not) Getting by in America*. Granta (2010).

Eisler, Riane. *The Real Wealth of Nations: Creating a Caring Economics*. Berrett-Koehler Publisher (2008).

Elson, Diane. 'Recognize, Reduce, and Redistribute Unpaid Care Work: How to Close the Gender Gap', *New Labor Forum* 26 (2) (2017): 52–61.

Estes, Nick. *Our History Is the Future*. Verso (2019).

Farris, Sara R, and Sabrina Marchetti. 'From the Commodification to the Corporatization of Care: European Perspectives and Debates', *Social Politics* 24 (2) (2017): 109–31.

France, David. *How to Survive a Plague: The Story of How Activists and Scientists Tamed AIDS*. Alfred A Knopf (2016).

Featherstone, David and Jo Littler. 'New Municipal Alternatives' (Special Issue), *Soundings: A Journal of Politics and Culture* 74, (2020).

Folbre, Nancy. *The Invisible Heart: Economics and Family Values*. New Press, (2001).

France, David. *How to Survive a Plague: The Story of How Activists and Scientists Tamed AIDS*. Alfred A. Knopf (2016).

Fraser, Nancy. *Fortunes of Feminism: From State-Managed Capitalism to Neoliberal Crisis*. Verso (2013).

Gibson-Graham, J. K. *The End of Capitalism (As We Knew It)*. Blackwell Publishers (2006).

Gilroy, Paul. *After Empire: Melancholia or Convivial Culture?*. Routledge (2004).

Graziano, Valeria, et al. *Rebelling with Care. Exploring Open Technologies for Commoning Healthcare*. WeMake (2019).

Gunaratnam, Yasmin. *Death and the Migrant: Bodies, Borders and Care*. Bloomsbury (2003).

Hakim, Jamie. *Work that Body: Male Bodies in Digital Culture*. Rowman & Littlefield International (2019).

Harvey, David. *Rebel Cities: From the Right to the City to the Urban Revolution*. Verso (2013).

Hill Collins, Patricia. *Black Feminist Thought: Knowledge, Consciousness, and the Politics of Empowerment*. Routledge (2000).

Himmelweit, Sue. 'The Discovery of "Unpaid Work": The Social Consequences of the Expansion of "Work"', *Feminist Economics* 1 (2) (1995): 1–19.

———. 'Care: Feminist Economic Theory and Policy Challenges', *Journal of Gender Studies Ochanomizu University* 16 (2013): 1–18.

Hochschild, Arlie. *The Outsourced Self: Intimate Life in Market Times*. Metropolitan Time (2012).

Hollway, Wendy. *The Capacity to Care: Gender and Ethical Subjectivity*. Routledge (2006).

Hudson, Bob. *The Failure of Privatised Adult Social Care in England: What Is to Be Done?*. CHPI (2016).

Klein, Naomi. *On Fire: The Burning Case for a Green New Deal*. Penguin (2019).

The LEAP Manifesto. leapmanifesto.org

Lebron, Christopher J. *The Making of Black Lives Matter: A Brief History of an Idea*. Oxford University Press (2017).

Liu, Jingfang, and Phaedra Pezzullo (eds). *Green Communication and China: On Crisis, Care and Global Futures*. University of Michigan Press (2020).

Littler, Jo. *Against Meritocracy: Culture, Power and Myths of Mobility*. Routledge (2020).

Lynch, Kathleen, John Baker and Maureen Lyons. *Affective Equality: Love, Care and Injustice*. Palgrave Macmillan (2009).

Moore, Jason and Raj Patel. *A History of the World in Seven Cheap Things*. Verso (2019).

Nava, Mica. *Visceral Cosmopolitanism: Gender, Culture and the Normalisation of Difference*. Berg (2007).

New Economics Foundation. *Co-operatives Unleashed*, neweconomics.org (2018).

Parker, Rozsika. *Torn in Two: The Experience of Maternal Ambivalence*. Virago (1995).

Pettifor, Ann. *The Case for the Green New Deal*. Verso (2019).

Pirate Care Collective. *Pirate Care Syllabus*, syllabus.pirate.care (2020).

Ratzka, Adolf. *Independent Living and Our Organizations: A Definition*. independentliving.org (1997).

Raworth, Kate. *Doughnut Economics: Seven Ways to Think like a Twenty-First-Century Economist*. Oxford Academic (2018).

Razavi, Shahra and Silke Staab (eds). *Global Variations in the Political and Social Economy of Care: Worlds Apart*. Routledge (2012).

Roberts, Dorothy. *Killing the Black Body: Race, Reproduction and the Meaning of Liberty*. Vintage (2000).

Roseneil, Sasha and Shelley Budgeon. 'Cultures of Intimacy and Care Beyond the Family: Personal Life and Social Change in the Early Twenty-First Century', *Current Sociology* 52(2) (2004): 153–9.

Rottenberg, Catherine. *The Rise of Neoliberal Feminism*. Oxford University Press (2019).

Rowbotham, Sheila, Lynne Segal and Hilary Wainwright. *Beyond the Fragments: Feminism and the Making of Socialism*. Merlin (2010).

Roy, Arundhati. 'The Pandemic Is a Portal', *YesMagazine*, 17 April.

Sassen, Saskia. *Losing Control? Sovereignty in the Age of Globalization*. Columbia University Press (2015).

Segal, Julia. *The Trouble with Illness: How illness and Disability Affect Relationships*. Jessica Kingsley Publishers (2017).

Segal, Lynne. *Out of Time: The Pleasures and Perils of Ageing*. Verso (2013).

———. *Radical Happiness: Moments of Collective Joy*. Verso (2017).

Shiva, Vandana. *Oneness vs the 1%: Shattering Illusions, Seeding Freedom*. New Internationalist (2018).

Skeggs, Beverley. 'What Everyone with Parents Is Likely to Face in the Future', *Sociological Review*, 29 March 2019, thesociologicalreview.com.

———. 'Values Beyond Value? Is Anything beyond the Logic of Capital?', *The British Journal of Sociology*, 65(1) (2014): 1–20.

Srnicek, Nick. *Platform Capitalism*. Polity (2016).

Tronto, Joan. *Caring Democracy: Markets, Equality, and Justice*. New York University Press (2013).

Vitale, Alex S. *The End of Policing*. Verso (2017).

Weissman, David. *We Were Here*. Peccadillo Pictures (2011).

Weston, Kath. *Families We Choose: Lesbians, Gays, Kinship*. Columbia University Press (1991).

White, Alan. *Shadow State: Inside the Secret Companies Who Run Britain*. OneWorld (2016).

Women's Budget Group *Crises Collide: Women and Covid-19*, wbg.org.uk (2020).

Yuval-Davis, Nira, Georgie Wemyss and Kathryn Cassidy. *Bordering*. Polity Press (2019).